# THE LAW of BUSINESS ATTRACTION

## Secrets of Cooperative Success

See Pg 39

presented by Ruby Yeh

Yinspire Media
info@yinspiremedia.com
www.YinspireMedia.com


Printed in the United States of America

ISBN 978-0-9819708-5-1

Editorial Director: AJ Harper
Print Management: The Book Lab
Cover Design: Pearl Planet Designs
Book Design & Typesetting: Thomas Keppel

www.LawOfBusinessAttraction.com

# Contents

# Foreword

## by Berny Dohrmann

A revolution is happening at this very moment — a revolution that calls on individuals, businesses, communities and even countries to turn away from competition and move toward cooperation and collaboration. Those who have joined this movement have attracted extraordinary opportunities and manifested outstanding results in their businesses, and have attained an unparalleled level of joy and satisfaction with their work.

The belief that goods and services would rise in quality and reach the masses faster through competitive processes is the great lie. In truth, competition squashes innovation and retards productivity.

Think of competition as a pyramid, where the people at the top push down on the people at the bottom with punishment and fear. In the center of the pyramid is exploitation. Now, imagine a wheel representing cooperation, where management is the hub collaborating with the spokes to create momentum in the wheel. Whether it is in a dentist's office or a Fortune 500 company, when all players work together, the center of the wheel is celebration. We spend our whole lives working — who wants to work in punishment and fear when we could be working in celebration?

---

*The belief that goods and services rise in quality and reach the masses faster through competitive processes is the great lie. In truth, competition squashes innovation and retards productivity.*

---

The Law of Attraction is based on spiritual principles. Competitive enterprise is void of spirituality, whereas at the core of cooperative enterprise is the philosophy that celebrates humans as spiritual beings who are having a human experience. Because of that, everyone's worth and value are honored — allowing the Law of Attraction to manifest the common and cooperative intentions.

Working cooperatively allows people to bring in master manifestations: realizing truly remarkable visions and creating astounding successes that others would surely deem impossible.

The belief that humans are to be maximally exploited counters the Law of Attraction, and does not allow manifestation on any level. In that we are all energy fields, and all of us have different energy fields, if we step into cooperative enterprise, we step into alignment of those fields. When you step into energy alignment, you experience resonance. From this place of resonance you are able to create from a larger energy field of possibilities, inspirations and solutions to problems. Cooperation allows for this powerful alignment of energy fields. It is not just a movement; it is the most important revolution on the planet.

*Working cooperatively allows people to bring in master manifestations: realizing truly remarkable visions and creating astounding successes that others would surely deem impossible.*

The first revolution in modern times was the Industrial Revolution, which brought humans away from feudalism and spawned competitive capitalism. Karl Marx and the socialists recognized that competitive capitalism was a flawed system that created wage slaves and a failed distribution of goods and services to masses of people. In this second revolution, leaders tried to manufacture a corrective system — but it was built on competitive bureaucracy, which also led to unfair distribution of wealth. This competitive system also disenfranchised masses of people, often in a worse way than competitive capitalism.

The third — and I believe final — revolution is the identification of competition as the mother of all viruses, and the implementation of cooperative organization and capitalism in the workplace. The authors in this book are the leaders of the most important revolution of the last 1,000 years — as important as the philosophy of Greece and the laws of Rome. This group is being forged within 140 countries, in the boardrooms of the biggest companies on earth that influence the greatest number of employees.

*Cooperation allows for this powerful alignment of energy fields. It is not just a movement; it is the most important revolution on the planet.*

Entrepreneurs, CEOs and community leaders are beginning to see that the problems we are experiencing cannot be solved by individuals motivated by self-interest, but only by the collective removal of competitive thinking and a collective celebration of cooperation — to the degree that the revolutionaries in this book have reached.

It is through cooperation and collaboration that we achieve enlightened capitalism, attracting prosperity for the greatest numbers. Are you ready to join the revolution?

# Introduction

## by Ruby Yeh

Something attracted you to this book. Without knowing why, you were compelled to read it, to find out how this book could help you to realize all of the dreams you have long held dear.

The same force that attracted you to read this book will attract people to your business — investors, customers, employees, partners and champions of your business. How do you tap in to this force, the Law of Business Attraction? It begins with a simple but powerful paradigm shift in business methodology.

---

*What would you attract to your business and your life if you replaced competition with collaboration?*

---

What would happen if you stopped worrying about your competitors — real and imagined — and focused your energy on your own vision and passion? How would you feel about business if you never had to worry whether you were getting the better part of a deal, or how to stop other companies from encroaching on your market? What would you attract to your business and your life if you replaced competition with collaboration?

Last year I attended a business conference for CEOs and entrepreneurs in Los Angeles. After arriving at LAX, I rushed to the hotel to catch the evening sessions. When I arrived at the conference I was taken aback by the warm reception I received from everyone. There was an inclusive and uplifting vibe throughout the building. Everywhere I went people asked me what type of project I was working on, and offered to help me. In the elevators, in the hallways, in the trainings rooms, everyone was attentive to my ideas and embraced my presence.

Was this for real? Had I entered some sort of alternate universe? After two decades in the high-tech industry, the nurturing space seemed like an entrepreneur's version of Fantasy Island! As I became immersed in this open, inclusive and supportive environment I felt myself relax and let go. There was no need to rush anymore, no need to summon up an adrenaline rush in order to perform, stand out or compete. I was able to slow down, breathe and be truly present to the people and opportunities right there in front of me.

---

*What is it like to truly LIVE these principles, to operate according to these higher ideals?*

---

It was a revelation. I asked myself, why is that we don't do business like this all the time? Why do we persist in building systems based on competitiveness? It couldn't be because competition garners greater success. I eventually met countless individuals who, despite humble or "limited" circumstances, had climbed to the top of their own mountain by following a business model rooted in cooperation and collaboration. There is a great deal of talk about "teamwork," "co-opetition" (cooperating with competitors), and collaboration in business books and management philosophy. But until that fateful and inspiring conference, I had not seen many real examples of these theories put into action.

What is it like to truly LIVE these principles, to operate according to these higher ideals? I decided to find real examples of people who are dreaming, brainstorming and building cooperatively, people who are launching, operating and growing businesses collaboratively. In the pages of this book, you will find a suite of stories showcasing people who not only believe wholeheartedly in a cooperative approach to business, but who credit this methodology with attracting amazing business success. The visionaries in this book are really living it, doing it.

For many of the authors in this book, cooperation and collaboration just came naturally to them, without conscious effort. For others their involvement in this cooperative movement evolved from necessity, observation or wisdom — that "aha" moment that changes everything.

Compiling this book was a labor of love. Please join me on a journey, exploring the transformational power of a caring, cooperative, nurturing, collaborative and dynamic way of doing business. Each story, in its own unique way, is an opportunity for you to have your own "aha" moment. On behalf of the dozens of authors in this book, I thank you for sharing this fun adventure with us.

# A Testimony to Cooperative Business

## by Lisa Nichols

There is enough for everyone — period. There is enough success, wealth, food, recognition, joy and love for every single human being on earth.

When you get this, when you fully embrace this fundamental truth, you will experience the miracle of co-creation. Like the authors in this book, I have experienced this miracle time and time again. What an amazing gift it is to read their inspiring stories of revelation, transformation and accomplishment through cooperation.

*In collaboration we are co-creating, manifesting a shared vision in alignment with the universe — and the result is more than we would have achieved as individuals.*

As revealed in *The Law of Business Attraction*, when you work competitively, you work from an energy of scarcity and deprivation. When you work collaboratively, you work from an energy of sharing and abundance. Where energy goes, energy grows, and so working in collaboration with others attracts more abundance to you — more clients, more income, more strategic alliances and more fulfillment in your work.

Working with a self-first, competitive mindset tells the Universe that you do not believe that there is enough to go around. If you believe that there are limits, you are right. If you believe that there is an unlimited supply of *everything*, then you will always receive *more* than you need.

Always. In collaboration we are co-creating, manifesting a shared vision in alignment with the universe — and the result is more than we would have achieved as individuals.

Working from the knowing that "There is enough" allows us to capitalize on the synergy that is created only when we are operating as a group, a team, a family or a community. The saying, "Two move faster than one" is true, but what the saying really means is two *manifest* faster than one. A group of like-minded people working as co-creators — thereby aligning themselves with the Universe — can manifest at the speed of light!

---

*Collaboration is a choice. It is a way of being. It is a belief in limitless possibilities. When we work in the space of "There is enough" the Universe says, "I agree."*

---

Working cooperatively with people allows you to build on their strengths. You share ideas, energy, contacts and resources. It's a relationship built on mutual exchange. A re-lationship, like a re-lay race: someone has an idea, and then that idea sparks your idea, and then your idea sparks another idea and so on. This synergistic collaborative process will get you where you want to go much faster than working independently.

Operating from the belief that someone has to win and someone has to lose is such an unfortunate existence. Scarcity-based thinking leads to negative results; limitless thinking leads to positive results. The whole idea of cooperative dynamics shared in this book is that the energy is in the space of positivity, rather than negativity or deprivation. If you find yourself buying in to the myth of lack, take a step back and remember that it is just that — a myth. Collaboration is a choice. It is a way of being. It is a belief in limitless possibilities. When we work in the space of "There is enough" the Universe says, "I agree."

There is enough. Enough for every living soul on this planet to thrive. Enough for every dream to come true. Enough for the realization of every dream, the achievement of every goal and the fulfillment of every desire.

There is enough. Even for you.

*Known as "The Breakthrough Specialist," Lisa Nichols has reached millions worldwide with her message of empowerment, service, excellence and gratitude. Lisa is a dynamic speaker and founder of Motivating the Masses and* CEO *of Motivating Teen Spirit,* LLC. *Her participation in the self-development phenomenon,* The Secret, *catapulted Lisa's popularity across the globe. She has appeared on* The Oprah Winfrey Show, Extra, Larry King Live *and* NBC's *Emmy Award-winning show,* Starting Over.

*Through her groundbreaking program, Motivating Teen Spirit, Lisa has worked with more than 110,000 teens and prevented more than 3,000 suicides. She has been honored with many awards in recognition for her work, including the Humanitarian Award from South Africa, the Ambassador of Good Will Award, and the Emotional Literacy Award. Co-author of* Chicken Soup for the African American Soul *and* Chicken Soup for the African American Woman's Soul, *Lisa's best-selling new book* No Matter What *is an inspirational memoir that offers candid advice about how to develop the nine bounce-forward muscles that enable anyone to overcome any obstacle — no matter what!*

# How Big Is Your Playground?

T. HARV EKER

Money isn't everything, but when I was a kid, I believed it was. My parents came from Europe with nothing. They taught me that money was the key to my survival, so growing up all I wanted was to become rich.

I thought I'd be happy once I reached my goal, but instead I was depressed and dissatisfied. My solution was to become a Zen monk. After devoting myself to the study of Zen Buddhism, I expected to be happy at last. But I wasn't. Shifting my focus from making money to seeking enlightenment was an extreme move that made sense at the time, but I had allowed the pendulum to swing all the way to one side. I was out of balance.

---

*My playground became bigger and bigger and bigger until it was the size of the entire Universe.*

---

And then one day I received a message, which I wrote down on a post-it note: "Harv, embrace both parts of yourself." Of course! How obvious! In focusing solely on becoming wealthy I had ignored my spirit; and in focusing solely on spiritual study, I had ignored my monetary goals and financial wellness. I had been playing on a small playground, focused on one aim. When it hit me that I could do both, that I could blend heart and spirit with money and business, everything changed. My playground became bigger and bigger and bigger until it was the size of the entire Universe.

Once I learned to bridge the gap between spirit and business, I was able to change my mindset to accommodate my goal, letting go of the limiting thoughts that had prevented me from creating lasting and meaningful success. With my mind and energy focused on a unified purpose, happiness was inevitable, and from that ever-present joy came even more success. I started operating at a higher energy frequency, which allowed me to attract amazing opportunities and achieve extraordinary results.

*In focusing on your own mindset, you will identify your own gaps and build your own bridges, bridges that will serve as your path to success.*

As I teach in my Millionaire Mind Intensive trainings, the root of everything is thought process. Become the guardian at the gate of your mind. You cannot let disempowering thinking run your life. Catch negative thoughts before they take root — just say, "pass" or "cancel." No thought lives in your life rent-free; you are going to pay for every one of them.

In focusing on your own mindset, you will identify your own gaps and build your own bridges, bridges that will serve as your path to success. When your spirit and heart are aligned with your financial and business intentions, it is much easier to attract whatever you want. And you can accelerate that process through collaboration — by playing with like-minded colleagues, partners and friends.

The Law of Attraction is really the Law of Energy. If you want to play in the world in a big way, you will need a massive amount of energy moving toward that goal. Which means you need a lot more energy on your side of the field. A collaborative environment creates that; it allows more energy to be moving toward a specific result.

Energy is contagious. When you operate at a higher frequency, you will attract people to you. Surrounded by other people who also operate at a higher frequency, you will, together, attract the right people, in the right place, at the right time. To achieve certain things, to get things done in a bigger way and play on a bigger playground, you need more energy than you can put out on your own. Energy is either multiplied or reduced. If you are collaborative, you will increase the amount of energy going out toward your goal. If you are segmented, you will decrease the amount of energy going out toward your goal.

Going solo, there is only the "X" factor, which is your unique ability to achieve your goal. But it is also your limited amount of energy. (Even highly evolved, high-frequency individuals have a limited amount of energy.) If you have a partner, you have the "X" factor plus the "Y" factor. With more people on your team working toward a common goal, you continue to multiply the energy focused on your goal. This is how you will master and accelerate the Law of Attraction in your life and in your business.

---

*People forget why they are in business. By definition entrepreneurs, CEOS, or anyone in business is someone who solves problems for people for profit or pay.*

---

For example, I had a goal to find an executive experienced in the seminar business, but it was challenging to find someone who lived in or near our headquarters in Vancouver. Every time we brought on a new CEO or Marketing Director, he was from outside the industry. I kept thinking and saying, "Wouldn't it be amazing if we could get someone at the upper level with seminar experience?" Everyone on my team was focused on finding an executive with seminar experience, sending energy out into the Universe, unifying around our common goal.

Sure enough, we were able to attract someone with eighteen years' experience in the seminar business! Talk about the Law of Attraction, our new executive brought four other people from the industry with her in just four months. Now I have a slew of highly experienced people, the team I was asking for and *actively* searching for.

Sometimes the Law of Attraction works faster and more perfectly than you expect. Last year we decided to create communities in order to support people after our events. Too busy to spearhead the project myself, I knew I needed someone who could put together a community forum for us, someone so high level, he or she could do it without me. So I set the intention.

I spent Christmas with my family in Turks & Caicos. We had just finished building a condo there, and we wanted to make sure everything was in order. On the first day I ran to the grocery store for supplies. I was standing in the checkout line when out of nowhere this guy says, "Hi, Harv."

I was totally taken aback. I didn't know anyone on the island and I'd only been in Turks & Caicos for a few hours. "Do I know you?" I asked.

"I saw you speak in Singapore," he replied.

We chatted for a while. I learned that he lived on the island, and that he had ten people coming down for a visit who were looking for their next endeavor. "We just came off of a big project, building communities all over the world," he added. "What kind of communities?" I asked.

Oh, *exactly* the kind of community I was looking to build. Just like that, I found the person I needed to manage my project — in a grocery store on an island in Turks & Caicos! A few months later he started building our communities. Talk about lightning speed!

Do you see how in bridging the gap between spirit and business, and being open to collaborating with others to achieve my goals, I was able to attract the key people I needed to expand my playground even further? With a savvy executive with industry experience at the helm, we expanded our reach into different markets, expanded our customer base and expanded our revenue. We play big. And when our new communities get off the ground, we will expand our business even further.

People forget why they are in business. By definition entrepreneurs, CEOs, or anyone in business is someone who solves problems for people for profit or pay. Your job is to solve problems. If you come from there, the idea of being collaborative is much more approachable than if you are focused on other aims. Put it out there that you are willing to work with people, and make sure you are willing to do what it takes to be at a level where you can actually help. Otherwise, you are just a sponge, always taking. Give *first*.

The Universe is your playground, too. Your business can be off-the-charts successful and your life can be bigger, better and brighter than you ever dreamed possible. When you make the connection between spirit and business, your whole world opens up, and you start to see that you've been playing on the big playground all along. You just never noticed it. Sometimes the most obvious truths are the hardest to see.

What are your goals for your business? How far do you want to go? How big is your playground?

*Using the principles he teaches, T. Harv Eker went from zero to millionaire in only two-and-a-half years! Harv is the founder and president of Peak Potentials Training, the fastest growing personal development company in North America. His high-energy, cut-to-the-chase style keeps his audience spellbound. Harv's motto is "talk is cheap" and his unique ability is getting people to take action in the real world to produce real success. He has already touched the lives of over 500,000 people, helping them move closer to their goal of true financial freedom.*

*Harv is the author of the best-selling books* SpeedWealth *and* Secrets of the Millionaire Mind, *which went to Number 1 on* The New York Times, USA Today, *and* The Wall Street Journal *bestseller lists in the first month of publication. He has also developed several highly-acclaimed courses such as The Millionaire Mind Intensive, Life Directions, Wizard Training and Train the Trainer. He is also the producer and trainer of the world-famous Enlightened Warrior Training, and he recently launched The Wealthy Warrior: How to Succeed in Today's Economy...No Matter What! To learn more about Harv and his dynamic, transformational events, please visit www.harveker.com, www.peakpotentials.com, www.millionairemind.com, and www.wealthywarrior.com.*

# The 360-Degree Win

KIMBER LIM

Name your destiny. Right now, before you read any further, name your destiny. Say it out loud. What is it that you were meant to do? If you were living the highest version of yourself, what would your life look like? Who would you be?

More importantly, how will the world benefit when you fulfill your destiny? How will your family, your community, your country — the *earth* — be better off *because* you took the ultimate risk and met your destiny head on?

We are entering the age of the humanitarian, a time when masses of people will risk living their lives for the highest good. As advocates of and participants in cooperative business, we are custodians of economic transformation. In this new age, our dreams will be in alignment with our highest purpose, with who we are destined to become. Our dreams will be bigger and bolder, rooted in a desire to create dynamic, positive change on the planet. And our dreams will serve the collective, producing the *greatest* good for the *most* people — including ourselves.

I am an indomitable warrior for living out my destiny, which is to aid in personal transformation for the good of humanity. It is my calling, my HIGHEST purpose. I use business as a venue for transforming lives, because if you are going to make a difference on the planet, commerce is a great way to do it. Whether they realize it or not, every person carries within them a passionate dream waiting to be fulfilled, and that dream is a key to unlocking each person's highest purpose. I've worked with thousands of entrepreneurs, and I've never met anyone who couldn't be coached to name her destiny (and it rarely has to do with the goals or deal we are hammering out together).

I began my career in banking working with a developer on a multi-million dollar project. The quality of our professional relationship took a quantum leap when I asked him what inspired him to be in business. In discovering that inspiration together, we began to carve out how we would *collaborate* together. We had created a bridge; we had begun building trust and genuine respect for one another. And we were able to align in a direction that fueled a "yes" for both of us, a "yes" that would make his dream a reality.

*I am an indomitable warrior for living out my destiny, which is to aid in personal transformation for the good of humanity. It is my calling, my* HIGHEST *purpose. I use business as a venue for transforming lives, because if you are going to make a difference on the planet, commerce is a great way to do it.*

Collaboration in alignment yields impressive results, but successful collaboration depends on ensuring that everyone involved gets that "yes," that everyone gets a win. That's just common sense, but it's also just the basic premise. We need to dig deeper to achieve the level of collaboration that attracts massive success in business. To get a 360-degree win, in which each collaborator — including you — gets a win, the destiny of each individual must be crystal clear. If you are unsure of your destiny, then you won't get your win. When you are clear about your higher purpose, you can easily and quickly determine if your proposed collaboration is in alignment with that purpose, thereby giving you the win you need to say "yes."

Dreams are at the heart of every deal. Always start with the dream; the details can be worked out later. In fact, the details of the collaboration mean nothing unless everyone involved is aligned with common purpose *and* in support of the dream of each person. If you want to attract amazing opportunities and big results, you have to want that for others, for everyone on your team. This is the alchemic formula for creating "gold" in business. After bridging the gap, learning the dreams of your partners or associates and determining that there is a true alignment of vision, you will be able to achieve a win all around, a 360-degree win. If you sense that a potential collaborator is not aligned with you, or not up to the work, set them free. Let them go so that they may seek their own 360-degree win.

Time is of the essence. Momentum is essential when attracting results in business, and in life. You will accomplish your mission if you are working with those who are a good fit, so don't waste time trying to "make it work" with someone who is not. You may feel a kinship with someone, or great admiration for someone, but that is not enough to make a collaboration work beautifully, effortlessly and dynamically.

Coming from finance, I've made a lot of people money. In the past, when I didn't define the 360-degree win, my clients made a lot of money off of other people's backs. But their lives didn't work, and I was not fulfilled because I was not living up to my destiny. Remember, the 360-degree win includes YOU. When you take your destiny out of the equation "for the good of the project," you end up just serving people all day long. You have to stand for having it all, for being in the foreground of your own life.

When I named and claimed my destiny, I began to attract clients who were in perfect alignment with me. Now, when we come together, I ask clients to tell me about their business. Within two minutes, I know if it's a hit, if it's aligned with my purpose. Then, once we get working, there is open space for creativity. People are lit up and excited by this alignment — it's when ideas and opportunities start showing up. Once my clients are educated and inspired about what is really important — their highest purpose — they have what they need to bust through. When you play small, you hold yourself up. I've worked with newbie entrepreneurs and I've worked with billionaires, and this is true for everyone, regardless of circumstance.

It is much easier to attract capital when everyone is on the same mission. It is also easier to attract capital when the dream is huge; scaling down your dreams in order to appear more reasonable or worthy is a strategy that backfires. For example, I have a quiet, reserved client in the tech industry. Five years ago he came to me with the goal of starting a business. The goal was doable, but was it his destiny? I challenged him to dream big, REALLY big, so big it would seem outrageous to everyone, including him. I explained that the "how" is not relevant, only the "what" and the "why." The "what" is the dream, and the "why" is your higher purpose. He thought for a moment and then blurted out, "I will be awarded a billion-dollar project within five years." He surprised himself with that bold, big statement. But he did it. Not in five years — he landed his billion-dollar project in under four years!

*To get a 360-degree win, in which each collaborator — including you — gets a win, the destiny of each individual must be crystal clear. If you are unsure of your destiny, then you won't get your win.*

The business world is full of similar stories: people who challenged themselves to go deeper, farther, higher — to go beyond the daydream and claim their true destiny. One of my favorite client stories is about Mai Lieu, a brilliant inventor who came to me with the desire to be recognized and taken seriously as a leader. Once we established that her destiny was to create a House of Brands empire, she upped her game. In aligning with her highest vision for her life, she was ready to collaborate with me to create phenomenal results, fast. When you start from the scariest, must "unattainable" dream, amazing things happen. In less than two years Mai went from the idea stage to licensing her first product, the CreaClip/Trimperfect, which sold out every time it showed on the Home Shopping Network (HSN).

Mai is on track to generate five million in sales this year, has created two new products, has been featured in many national magazines and television programs and was a finalist for the Stevie Award for "Best New Product of the Year."

Destiny is a powerful word. Naming your destiny can seem daunting; it's much easier to declare a dream, an idea, a goal or an aspiration. Some dreams may never materialize, but destiny is inevitable. That's big, scary stuff. Have the courage to go HIGHER than your dreams and claim your rightful place on this planet.

If you want to attract extraordinary outcomes for your business and your life, go for the 360-degree win. Name your destiny and collaborate with others who have done the same, and who are in alignment with your highest purpose. Start with the impossible, not with what is reasonable, acceptable or "doable." The life you lead and the footprint you leave is equally as important as the success you achieve.

*The life you lead and the footprint you leave is equally as important as the success you achieve.*

Once you have claimed your destiny and your collaborators are in place, the rest is pure fun and great rewards, rewards that will transform your life in ways you have not imagined — yet!

*Kimber Lim is the director of Transformational Business, a firm committed to transforming business, leaders and results through top-level mentoring, sequential coaching and a host of other products and services. Kimber starts with the life of your biggest, boldest imagination and builds a solid platform on which to navigate those results into reality. Transformational Business strengthens values-oriented leaders and companies, helping them create footprints that impact their own lives, communities and the world. The firm generated over one billion in sales for a publicly traded firm, and recently assisted in creating a start-up company with no cash that sold for fifty-two million dollars in less than four years.*

*Kimber is publisher and co-founder of* Savant Professional Success Journal *and co-founder of Target Media Now Group, LLC. She holds a Bachelor's degree in Applied Economics from USF, and a Master's degree in Management and Organizational Behavior from John F. Kennedy University and the NTL institute. A renowned public speaker and a former professor at both the University of San Francisco College of Professional Studies and the Stanford Graduate School of Business, Kimber has taught more than 3,500 executives and provided one-on-one training for more than 7,200 entrepreneurs.*

*Building on more than twenty-five years of experience in the business world with an emphasis in sales, banking, finance and real estate, Kimber is co-creator and leader of the popular Women of the World coaching series, which helps women embrace their femininity, beauty and power with grace. Kimber was voted one of California's Top 50 Business Women in 2004. She is currently working on her next book, which will be available in 2010. To learn more about Kimber and her firm, visit www.transformationalbusiness.com and www.transformationalwomen.com.*

# The Power of Possibilities

DR. MELISSA ANDERSSON

*"Never doubt that a small group of thoughtful, committed people can change the world. Indeed, it is the only thing that ever has."*

Many of us recognize this simple, powerful quotation from the famous anthropologist Margaret Mead. But how many of us truly believe these words — or know how to put them into practice? The potential for peace, prosperity, joy and empowerment for everyone on this magnificent planet of ours is endless. Together, we have the power to make positive change on levels we've barely begun to imagine.

It is our own personal transformations that ready us for true, heartfelt engagement with the rest of the world. Our own empowerment creates such great abundance within our lives that it naturally spills over into others' lives. And it is our own joy and fulfillment that make it possible to genuinely connect with others in "paying it forward" and acting cooperatively — with a whole wide world in mind.

We've seen how it is possible to take our challenges and difficult experiences and turn them into pure proactivity. Our growing awareness of the importance of safeguarding human rights, for example, has caused the creation of thousands of grassroots organizations and cooperative communities. These movements have forever changed human history. And it wouldn't be possible without individual commitment to healing.

Harnessing the power of our human potential to work together and help each other is my life's work. And what a journey it's been! When I was nine years old, my parents divorced. Mom and I moved to Selma,

Alabama, just weeks after "Bloody Sunday." People were being murdered there just for being black. White people were killed or brutalized for trying to help them. I was traumatized by the suffering and violence all around me. Even though Mom worked day and night at two different jobs, we had barely enough money to get by. Virtually alone in a world I didn't understand, I didn't know how I would survive — or regain any hope for my future.

One thing I did have, though, was a library card. I began reading voraciously. Through a difficult adolescence, I read about psychology, personal growth, natural medicine and spiritual perspectives. I drew hope and inspiration from biographies of great leaders and pioneers, especially those who had overcome dire circumstances and gone on to make important contributions to humanity. Many of them were very strong, independent characters, but none of them could have done it alone. At every step of the way, a chance meeting or a strong connection propelled these extraordinary lives.

*Harnessing the power of our human potential to work together and help each other is my life's work. And what a journey it's been!*

As I read, worlds began to open. Eventually, they opened faster than my trauma responses could close them. Books had awakened me to a sense of my own power and potential. As I clung to hope for my future, some of the pain and fear I felt transmuted into a sense of purpose and possibility. But I still had a long way to go in my own healing. Fear and subconscious programming are at the root of what holds us back from abundance, great relationships, glowing health, contagious joy and phenomenal success.

Often, our greatest fear is to look deep inside. However, it's essential. Embracing the fear deep within us *also* leads us to the place where what I call "miracle frequencies" live: laughter, joy, purpose, human connection, inspiration, hope — all those powerful energies that, when harnessed, help us break free of our fears and self-doubts and finally emerge as powerful, joyful beings. Those energies, once freed, manifest wonderful experiences and connections.

I've never called myself fearless, but many years ago I committed to embracing my fears. Step by step, choice by choice, this process has spurred the deepest transformations I have experienced, building a meaningful life that I love. It has attracted some of the most extraordinary people on the planet into my life, people who form the scaffolding of my collaborative humanitarian and professional network.

*Often, our greatest fear is to look deep inside.*
*However, it's essential.*

I always had an inclination to see the world and connect with people whose experiences were very different from my own. After years of reading about other countries and cultures, I was hired to work on a cruise ship at the age of twenty-two. It was a little scary, to be sure — I'd stepped out of the familiar and into my true element: passionate, joyful adventure.

I had a tiny room on board ship, but the rest of my world was vast. In every port, I'd leave the ship to sit down and talk with the local people. I faced my fear — and wouldn't you know it? I had a blast. I worked on a number of ships over the years. Cooperation and mutual respect created a wonderful setting for all of us. My shipmates were from all over the world. Many of them were from countries in conflict with one another. In the crowded, inescapably intimate environments of the ships, cooperation, respect, integrity and honesty were essential to every interaction. Because we made the effort to rise to the occasion — and it worked! — we called ourselves "mini United Nations." Today, I call what we created "co-supportive worlds."

These experiences were huge. I was deeply touched by the conscious, mutual effort it took for all of us, with all our potential barriers to understanding, to get along, have fun and do our work so that everything ran smoothly on the ships. Because I intuitively found fun ways of team-building amongst my ship-friends, I was often called the "Cruise Director for the Crew." Eventually, though, it was time to leave the cruise ships and pursue larger dreams.

I knew there must be bigger, better ways to spread empowerment, healing, happiness, peace, prosperity and success on a global level. I read, researched and studied healing and empowerment modalities that addressed the "whole person" — in mind, body and spirit. I was energized by my discoveries of fast, effective ways to tap into the innate intelligence of the mind and body and clear subconscious blocks to health, collaboration and success.

My passion for helping others led me to volunteer work, using natural medicine and trauma relief with people in need. I traveled to Mexico; to post-9/11 New York City, helping doctors through PTSD; and to India, working with Tibetan refugees in a climate of nuclear threat from Pakistan. Fear, in these settings, was natural, given the ever-present threats of disease and attack. But something happened when I witnessed the miracles of healing that took place. I was catapulted into a zone of possibility, my endurance heightened by the strength, love and gratitude of the people I worked with. To do my part to help placed me exactly where I wanted to be: in a cycle of healing and heartfelt connection with others. My fear transformed into a sense of immense gratitude for these amazing experiences.

In the midst of my travels, I made a huge turning-point business decision. The terrible poverty I'd witnessed in India made me shout to myself, "How *dare* I not make more money?" I'd been in private practice for years, but now I knew I had to reach more people — who could help more people.

I studied creative business systems and located cooperative business communities. I continued speaking to and coaching groups as a positive breakthrough specialist. Today, I'm in touch with thousands of people who are working to break through and become successful on every level. When they discover the joy of their authentic selves, they are moved to give back.

In order to accelerate the power of possibilities, we need to let go of what is holding us back. Feelings of lack or unworthiness not only rob us of our own lives; they also risk our potential to connect meaningfully with others and make a difference in the world. It's wonderful to witness the shift that occurs when people in my seminars clear detrimental inner programs and connect with their inner power. When people are uplifted in consciousness of their own wellness and abundance, they have great power to uplift others.

As we release our fears, our doubts and our subconscious beliefs about ourselves, we tap into the magic within. Thus, we energize the web of life and awaken the power of possibilities, unstoppable in our missions in cooperative communities of caring.

*Based in Florida, Dr. Melissa Andersson is a positive breakthrough specialist, peak performance trainer and international speaker. She is a Certified Mental Health Traumatologist, a Certified Pastoral Counselor, a Certified Hypnotist and a Certified Firewalk Instructor. She draws from a background as a Doctor of Natural Medicine (with focus on how the mind affects the body). She is a specialist in stress relief, team-building, energy medicine and kinesiology. She sets people on a quantum course of the "Human Possible" — laughing, joyous and in awe of their own capacities. www.humanpotentialcentral.com*

# Driving toward Success

SHERITA J. HERRING

Before you master the Law of Business Attraction, you must first understand your *personal* law of attraction.

"Driving toward Success" relates to a bus metaphor I often use in my public speaking, and in managing my life. Imagine a city bus, jam-packed with all the people you know as passengers — spouse, children, siblings, cousins, colleagues, neighbors, business associates and others. That's a crowded bus! But here's the key: you are the driver, and you decide who rides and where they sit.

One of the key characteristics of someone who successfully harnesses the Law of Business Attraction is motivation through passion, not profit. When your motivation is based on passion, you attract like-mindedness, positive energy and prosperity. What's amazing about the bus is, its seats are unlimited — so it never fills up. And your ability to maneuver your passengers and their seating positions is boundless.

When you are operating from your passion, people and situations are purposefully placed directly in your path. Case in point: once I was headed to Kansas City for a speaking engagement. I had been playing phone tag with a senator who was going to open at the event. Before traveling, I had other errands, and at one point I found myself standing in the back of a long line at the bank. I happened to have a stack of flyers with me, advertising my upcoming grant-related speaking engagement. While I waited, I turned over a flyer to write some notes on the back. The woman in front of me saw the word "grants" printed on the flyer in large letters. She asked for a copy, inquiring about grants and the event. Our conversation caught the attention of the woman behind us.

"Did you say you were going to Kansas City?" she asked. I told her yes, and that I was having difficulty contacting the senator who was to speak before me. She asked the senator's name, and I told her. She pulled out her cell phone, dialed and handed me the phone a few moments later. "Someone wants to talk to you," she said. To my surprise, it was the senator. She was the senator's niece. That's not coincidence, that's providence!

A lot of the time, life doesn't unfold that easily. So you'll also need to cultivate the next characteristic that drives my Law of Business Attraction: being astute in developing and nurturing relationships to further your cause. In other words, find out the strengths and weaknesses of those around you; know your own abilities and inabilities to figure out where, as a result, people belong — and let them go there. It's okay to let people be who they are. It's necessary.

---

*What's amazing about the bus is, its seats are unlimited — so it never fills up. And your ability to maneuver your passengers and their seating positions is boundless.*

---

I move people around on my bus all the time. For instance, I once had a prominent client who did not honor our contract. I lost thousands of dollars as a result of working hard and strengthening his business. I was so angry with him that I began proceedings to sue. Just as I was about to go public with his unethical actions, my long-time mentor (another prominent city official) stopped me. "You don't want to do this; it's not in your character," he said. "There's a better strategy. Find a way to make the relationship work for you. There's nothing wrong with using, it's misusing that's bad." I decided not to sue. I placed that client back by the emergency door of my bus, meaning I no longer allowed him to freely circulate in my immediate business circles.

But keeping the door of communication open with him did create opportunities for other relationships to develop and flourish. For instance, I spent months trying to get a meeting with an influential woman in my community, but she wouldn't give me the time of day.

Then, one afternoon, while I was in a meeting with the person who had wronged me, that same woman wanted to speak with him. He told her, "I'm in a private meeting with Ms. Herring." To her, my value was immediately amplified. I had no problem getting a meeting after that. In fact, *she* called *me*.

I often have to remind myself, "It's still my bus (my life)." So, whether I know them in a business or personal sense, I keep all those I'm not so comfortable with way in the back by the emergency door until I'm ready to interact with them. Then, when I want to have a conversation, or when I see these people at meetings or dinner parties, I'm in control of the situation. When I'm ready to use these contacts, I visualize myself adjusting my rearview mirror and allowing them to walk up the aisle to a closer seat. When the dealings are done, it's back to the emergency door for them.

It's a real trick, learning where to seat people on your bus. It's an acquired skill. Part of that skill is sensing when to let *life* dictate where people will be seated. When you're operating from your passion, God will place people where they need to be. You just have to sort of let it go, and let it happen.

---

*You can tell the character of a person by noting what it takes to upset him. To use the bus metaphor: Are you a road rage driver, or the kind who politely yields to others?*

---

Nobody is going to keep his same seat on the bus forever. Maybe your business partner needs to move on or has other interests; it's time for him to move back a seat or two. Maybe an old friend just became a new love interest, shifting from seat twelve to seat one. The important thing to remember is that all this moving around requires management skills, communication skills, patience and tolerance.

Then there are those important people who haven't boarded yet. To identify them, you need to know your ultimate goal and always be committed to it — another key to the Law of Business Attraction. I often imagine people I haven't yet met getting on my bus, people I need to advance my business. I envision them waiting at a stop ahead. Identifying them, I can map out strategies for success.

For those of you just getting started in cooperative business, the prospect of all this networking can be daunting. I understand completely. Take a deep breath, look around and see that your bus is already full. Now you just have to make sure that your passengers aren't in the wrong seats. Maybe it's been a while since you've spoken with some of the characters on your bus. Engage with your personal and professional networks. Reacquaint yourself with old friends, reignite old alliances, nurture current relationships and mend wounded ones. Then you can decide where everyone belongs on your bus, and networking will become effortless. You'll soon develop positive passengers for prosperity.

As driver, there is one rule I never break: I never kick anyone off my bus. No matter what people may have done, you never know when you might need them again. Another key to the Law of Business Attraction is the capacity to overcome obstacles. I don't care how good a driver you are — at some point you are going to make a wrong turn. Wouldn't it be a shame if the one person who could provide the direction you need is the very one you kicked off years ago, because she caused you pain or anger? It would not only be a shame; it could be detrimental, even fatal to your business. No matter the pain or circumstance, I've found a way to place the offender where I need him to be through forgiveness, patience and tolerance.

You can tell the character of a person by noting what it takes to upset him. To use the bus metaphor: Are you a road rage driver, or the kind who politely yields to others? I can't ever overlook how much being my own life's driver has taught me how to laugh, even when I wanted to cry. Laughter is invaluable. It's good for the soul. If you err in your decision making, it's important not to let it get you down. My business acumen and personal growth were acquired by my life's journey on my bus. The twists and turns, relationships, accomplishments and disappointments are all part of the journey.

*As driver, there is one rule I never break: I never kick anyone off my bus. No matter what people may have done, you never know when you might need them again.*

When driving your own bus, you have to believe in your abilities. This may be the most important characteristic connected with the Law of Business Attraction. My motto, which I constantly say to others and myself, is YAYOL (pronounced yah-yoal) — "You Are Your Only Limitation." On my bus, and in my life, I am my only limitation. I have the power to create situations for growth and prosperity, both personally and professionally. I also have the ability to decide who rides on my bus and where they sit. The great thing is, so do you!

*Sherita J. Herring is the Founder and CEO of the Kreative Images Foundation (KIF). She is a radio personality and community and economic development strategist whose ultimate passion is helping others. She is continuously focused on strengthening businesses by providing quality, professional and unique business coaching all over the world.*

*Additionally, Sherita is a sought-after motivational speaker. She has received countless awards and honors for her altruistic efforts, which include launching the first national housing database for victims of Hurricane Katrina, establishing programs in underdeveloped places like Africa, China and the Philippines and motivating prisoners within the California prison system.*

# The Next Level

PATRICK SMYTH

For several years now I have been concerned that my teenage son would not easily develop into a fully functioning adult man. From the age of about fourteen he changed.

I knew him to be intelligent and articulate. Suddenly he appeared incapable of what I considered to be normal human communication. A series of grunts, monosyllables and shrugs of the shoulder seemed to be all he could muster. He could use this method to meet his basic needs of food, shelter and, of course, his game console and computer. For the most part, this has been his mode of communication for a few years now. If you really want to hear him talk, ask him to tell you about his latest game. Not for us the easy and more familiar world of football scores or basketball plays. Our bonding moments these days occur over the tally of the number of kills he made, or the number of "golds" he earned or what level his latest character is on.

I have had to learn a new language in order to have a basic understanding of what occupies him for much of his time. To my anguish, he seemed destined for "super geek-dom." I could foresee him living a solitary life in front of a computer, tapping away at a virtual world, and disconnected from humankind. He'd be conducting raids on foreign lands, killing, being killed and then reviving himself at a keystroke to begin the game again.

His mother, too, was concerned about his grades, his future, his socialization skills and just how much he liked conquering others and killing his opponents. I reminded her that she sounded just like our grandparents did in the good old days. As kids, we didn't mind our manners; we talked too much or not enough. Left to our own devices we would run around outside pretending to be cops and robbers, killing each other, or being killed, and then being magically revived and "shooting" each other once again. Our weapons were fingers and sticks pointed at our targets, along with shouts of "POW!" and theatrical, award-winning dying sequences.

A far cry from the virtual reality point-and-click world? Perhaps. It seems that the more things change, the more they stay the same. Without stereotyping or generalizing, "Boys will be boys," you may say. It's our natural tendency to kill or be killed. Survival of the fittest. Dog eat dog. Game designers have tapped into this reality. Take a look at some of the titles in my son's game library; *Warhammer, Spore, Star Wars* (hey, I recognize that one!), *World of Warcraft, Dead Rising, Gears of War* and *Grand Theft Auto*, just to name a few. It's the way things are, whether in corporate America, on the inner-city streets or in countries torn by civil wars. In so many ways, the games are, in fact, a reflection of the "real" world.

Gamers get really good at raiding each other's worlds. They have trigger fingers that can hit that key so quickly you can't even see the movement. And when they play online with others, they get really smart about tactics. They learn to take orders from bosses, to collaborate with others to successfully complete their attacks and to wait their turn for rewards. The first time I heard that one, I wondered what happened to the old, "That's just not *fair*," complaint when measuring out how much soda he had compared with his older sister.

*It's the way things are, whether in corporate America, on the inner-city streets or in countries torn by civil wars. In so many ways, the games are in fact a reflection of the "real" world.*

Occasionally my son comes out with an Australian expression that he learned from someone called Bruce. He might say something in Japanese that he heard last night, or he'll say something about his friend in Holland. I've learned not to be surprised at anything he comes out with. It's when he speaks in a perfect Scottish accent that I check under the bed to see if there's anything there that might explain this amazing transformation. The answer is that he's chatting to real people, real Aussies, Japanese, Dutchmen or Scotsmen. There's no age difference, self-consciousness, race, gender, shyness or embarrassment in his virtual world. Everyone's on the same page, everyone has something in common. And — guess what — they are all talking to and cooperating with each other!

Being a concerned parent, I decided to do some research to see if I could understand his "condition." My mind was put somewhat at ease to find out that he was in the company of millions of others. The book by John C. Beck and Mitchell Wade titled *The Kids Are Alright: How the Gamer Generation Is Changing the Workplace* was a great help. If you have a teenage gamer or may be hiring young gamers, that book is a very helpful place to start.

Until now, success in his gaming world has been measured in body counts, size of territory and money in the bank. Not too dissimilar from the real world? In business, we'd all love to see the marketplace littered with the remains of our competitors. We'd love to be "king" of our territory. And of course, one of our major reasons for doing this is to put money in the bank. And how do we do this? We do it by strategizing, by raiding, then attacking and eliminating our opponents and ultimately reaping the rewards.

Over dinner recently, my son was quieter than usual. I knew that he'd bought a new video game, which he'd been playing for a few days. He said that the game had gone from super-easy and fun to ridiculously difficult. It had seemed so simple: "You get stuff and then do stuff, then you colonize space."

He explained that you start by choosing the environment you would like to grow in. You have a choice of forests, deserts, jungles, seashore and so on. Then you decide whether you are a carnivore, herbivore or omnivore. You get to choose personality traits like aggressive or collaborative. Your character is now ready to be born. You have great flexibility in this area as well, being able to assemble creatures with the most unlikely features and limb structure. Of course, you need to make selections based on the environment you have chosen so that you can feed and move about successfully.

Now you devour as much food as you can in your new domain and soon you stretch yourself beyond that to the world at large. All the while, your character is growing in strength almost regardless of the characteristics you had chosen at the start. You are successfully becoming the leader of your world. You now go to the next level — outer space. Suddenly you are faced with traveling to far away galaxies and meeting new strange creatures and conditions. All the tactics you learned from growing up in your home world no longer seem to work.

---

*There is no way to win in this game, or any significant game, without learning how to cooperate with others. That means developing skills that are helpful to others, and matching others' skills to your unique needs at any given time.*

---

My son's character was a very aggressive carnivore. He believed he needed to be the most powerful and awesome warrior he could be. He knew he would face many challenges. He was able to destroy and dominate anything that got in his way. By being the ultimate competitor, he became the conqueror of his world. Once he got to outer space, however, he found many situations that he was not well equipped to manage. Food sources were sapped away. As an aggressive character, he had an unusually large number of enemies and very few, if any, allies. It became clear to him very quickly that he had made a mistake. As a lone-wolf aggressor, he was not going to survive. He needed the talents and skills of other characters, and he needed to be more versatile himself. My son found, by experience, that there is no way to win in this game, or any significant game, without learning how to cooperate with others. That means developing skills that are helpful to others, and matching others' skills to your unique needs at any given time. Without the right collaborative, team building, cooperative spirit, you will simply fade away.

In business, three key elements must be aligned to create the potential for success. They are: 1) a compelling vision; 2) comprehensive strategies to execute that vision; and 3) committed leadership to achieve the vision and strategies.

As a father and as a businessman, I was thrilled that my son learned this powerful lesson at such a young age. Leading with this spirit of cooperation will unleash the potential and catapult the business forward — to the next level, and beyond!

*CEO of Innovation Habitude, Patrick Smyth is a leadership navigator and mentor focused on developing high-performing businesses through effective strategic planning, leadership and marketing. He connects visions with strategies and creates effective plans for achieving business goals. He provides advice to manage the roadmap successfully to build sustained productive growth. Patrick is an international advisor and board member to several small and high-growth companies.*

*Patrick completed the Leadership Program at Harvard Business School, the Leadership Development Program at the Center for Creative Leadership, the Steven Covey Principle Centered Leadership program, and is a certified Six Sigma Champion. His BS in Business Administration equivalent is through Seton Hall University and Bloomfield College in New Jersey, in addition to many company-sponsored education programs. Patrick is the author of* Elephant Walk: Balancing Business Performance and Brand Strategy for the Long Haul. *To learn more about Patrick, please visit www.innovationhabitude.com.*

# Is Your Business Invisible?

DAVID TYREMAN

In 1988, I started my first business, London Antique. With little money and no experience, I launched the company intending to supply antique and vintage display items to retailers and department stores. I quickly discovered that the market in California was entirely sewn up by one supplier, Vintage, Inc. Yet despite my perceived limitations, we attracted so much business that by 1990 the owner of Vintage, Inc. hired a private detective to follow me.

My rival was so incensed at our success he actually called one of my clients, Banana Republic, and tried to convince it to cancel its $200,000 contract with me. (It didn't work.) He told the company I was doing a terrible job and that he would do it for half the price, even if it meant taking a loss. And he used the information provided to him by the private detective to prove that he knew what he was talking about. (Sneaky, right?) Why was he so desperate, so willing to resort to spying and lying in order to compete for business? It was simple: unlike the other suppliers in the market, London Antique was not an imitation of Vintage, Inc. We were able to land order after large order from some of the biggest customers in the market because we created our own brand identity, which made us stand out; which made us visible.

Have you ever noticed that most plumbers seem like ... wait for it ... plumbers? That most realtors seem like other realtors, and that most major airlines seem just like other airlines? When you realize how often people and businesses in the same type of industry look and behave like everyone else, is it any wonder that it's so hard to be successful? Beware of this trap. Beware of joining the "club" that many otherwise intelligent people accidentally join, believing, "This is the way IT is done." When businesses and people behave like one another, they accidentally and inadvertently become INVISIBLE to their market.

It's human nature to want to fit in and feel a sense of belonging. So when people start a business or begin a new campaign to increase sales, they can't help looking to see how other people in their industry do it. The result is masses of businesses get lost in the quagmire of sameness, actually taking steps that are the equivalent of bolting on camouflage. How are you supposed to attract customers if no one can see you?

People love to choose businesses, products, services and other people that stand out. When you stand out from all of the others in your industry, you allow the Law of Attraction to operate at full speed. The secret is to build a brand identity that is authentic, unique to you, and that makes you feel inspired.

When I first started London Antique and learned about my biggest competitor, I felt inadequate and pretty worried about our future. Vintage, Inc. had dominated the market for years; it had a fifty-thousand-square-foot warehouse in New York, ten million dollars in inventory and salespeople all over the country. I, on the other hand, ran my little business from a four-hundred-square-foot garage in Southern California with about three thousand dollars in inventory. It was only my business partner and I trying to get sales, and we weren't very good at making sales.

---

*You may have actual competitors, but what do they have to do with your company? Why would you let other companies or the market that you are in define your brand identity?*

---

Initially, I believed that in order to get potential customers to take me seriously I would have to compete with Vintage, Inc. I would have to move my business out of my garage, and into a warehouse, just like Vintage. I would have to spend a fortune to increase my inventory and fill that warehouse, just like Vintage. And I would have to purchase trucks and hire employees for distribution, *just like Vintage*. I was wrong — I didn't have to do anything just like Vintage, Inc. I just had to identify what was authentically unique about my business and build from there.

Some businesses go to great lengths to mimic their competition, hoping to achieve a similar level of success. Some accidentally emulate other businesses in their industry because they assume it is standard practice. And others deliberately follow the status quo out of fear, fear that they will not be able to compete in the marketplace unless they look and act like other companies in their industry. All of that emulation detracts from what should be their real focus: creating an authentic brand identity. And that means developing an authentic presence in the market where your company is well positioned and well differentiated from all others. You may have actual competitors, but what do they have to do with your company? Why would you let other companies or the market that you are in define your brand identity?

Attracting masses of loyal customers is easier when you focus on building a brand Identity that is genuine, differentiated and relevant. When you direct your attention to creating your brand, your business becomes desirable — an easy, obvious choice. You can then charge what you deserve rather than what the market dictates. After all, if you look, feel and act just like everyone else you have no ability to charge any more than anyone else. Rather than ask, "Who is our competition and how do they do it?" ask, "Who are WE and WHY do we do it?" Build your brand identity from the heart and it will always stand out from the crowd.

I was still trying to figure out how to compete with Vintage, Inc. when I landed my first big order, antique beds for a Macy's store in southern California. The only reason I even got the order was that Vintage, Inc. was based on the East Coast and Patti, the buyer, didn't have time to wait for the shipment. I bribed my friends with pizza, hired a U-haul, and together we drove down to LA to deliver the order.

We had a lot of fun with Patti and the Macy's staff and stayed to help set up the displays. The deal was such a success that it gave me the courage to ask Patti why they chose to do business with us instead of Vintage, Inc. or another supplier. "Because you're fun and I like you," Patti replied. She went on to explain that she hated Vintage, Inc. because the employees were rude and careless and routinely messed up orders.

Patti's response rocked my world. The competitor I had imagined to be perfect, the competitor I thought I had to beat, was suddenly reduced to something I did not need to compete with at all. We were already a more desirable choice simply by being ourselves. From that point on everything changed because I understood that Patti was not buying antiques and vintage items from me, she was buying an experience — a fun, thoughtful, sincere experience.

*You may believe that you have to compete with other businesses for the same customers, but in reality, your customers are yours and yours alone. Differentiate your brand identity, and you will own your marketplace.*

From that point on my behavior changed. Instead of worrying about what size my garage was or how much inventory I had, I focused on the experience we offered our customers, making sure they felt absolutely great about doing business with my company. We were on our way, at the very beginning of creating our own unique authentic brand identity. The more we focused on building that identity, the more business mushroomed.

London Antique grew and grew. Customers told me they lived vicariously through the adventure we were having in growing our business, meaning they actually *loved* that we did not look or act like Vintage, Inc. with its massive warehouse and inventory. By being ourselves, we maintained a presence that stood out in the market, which allowed us to attract amazing clients and opportunities. From that little garage we grew to become a multi-million dollar success story featured on CNN and other TV shows, in *The Wall Street Journal* and in hundreds of other magazines and newspapers.

You may believe that you have to compete with other businesses for the same customers, but in reality, your customers are yours and yours alone. Differentiate your brand identity, and you will own your marketplace. Competing does not work with the Law of Attraction; competitiveness is a trap that robs you of your individuality. The way to let go of the competitive model is to re-define competition. In truth, your biggest competition is not another company; it is indifference in the marketplace. When people are indifferent to you, or when they don't know who you are or what you stand for, they are not likely to become your customers. So in all reality, your biggest competitor is YOU.

Give yourself permission to be authentic, to be yourself. Put it all out there, the whole truth and nothing but the truth. What you attract when you are genuine are customers who want to work with *you*, collaborators who want to work in cooperation with *you*, and investors who want to put their money behind *you*; the *real* you.

When you know who you are and you present a clear, differentiated, relevant brand identity, you attract customers without effort. Your ideal customers see you and they connect with you immediately. They just show up wanting exactly what you have to offer. (And they never doubt you, even when your biggest competitor tells them they should!)

There is greatness inside of you — and that greatness could also be ahead of you, if you dare to be VISIBLE.

*Author of* World Famous: How to Give Your Business a Kick-Ass Brand Identity, *David Tyreman has collaborated with some of the best-known brands on the planet. David started his business in his garage and turned it into a multi-million dollar powerhouse, attracting clients such as Nike, Disney, Polo Ralph Lauren, Tommy Hilfiger, Banana Republic, Macy's and Old Navy. He has been featured on* CNN, *and in numerous publications, including* The Wall Street Journal *and the* Los Angeles Times. *A sought-after facilitator and speaker, David reveals his proven techniques for creating an authentic, magnetic brand identity in his World Famous* DVD *training series. To learn more about David and his revolutionary Campaign for Individuality, visit www.world famouscompany.com.*

# Transcending Gender, Age & Race Barriers

RUBY YEH

I have this cool little game I like to play. It sometimes drives my friends crazy.

I am always trying to figure out what someone's passion is. I ask, "What really matters to you?" or "What hidden talents would you like to cultivate?" This is usually when my friends groan because I want to start strategizing with them about how they can go for their dreams and they usually just want to kick back and chill out. But I love it. I'm fascinated by what is in someone's heart, the secret wishes that lie buried deep inside. I guess I have been playing this game in business for a long time, though not in such a direct way.

When I started my high tech career back in the 1980s, I was among the hordes of bright-eyed young women who were happily surfing the fast-rising waves of the economic boom in the Boston Technology Corridor. We all dressed alike: dark suits, big shoulder pads and the silk bow ties, which was the de rigueur corporate uniform for women at the time. We were taught the same business strategies: outwit, outrun and outperform the competition. And we all had barriers to overcome: gender, age and, in my case, race. But I didn't worry or even think about any of that.

I was simply thrilled to have a position that promised loads of travel and the opportunity to work with a diverse and smart group of people. It turned out to be the perfect environment for me to play my game. As an International Marketing Manager, I reported directly to the Senior VP of Asia/Pacific. I was the advocate for him and all the Country Managers, and my job was to be their eyes and ears at the two-thousand-person headquarters. It was a fantastic job because I got to freely traverse all ranks and departments.

I caught the entrepreneurial fever when I became the second in command for the newly formed international division of a start-up software company. Sitting on a boatload of venture capital, our company gave us the directive to open and penetrate the international market. My main roles were to find and select international distributors and to support the new subsidiaries. In less than four years we established seven subsidiaries and a dozen distributors, growing the International Division's annual revenue from zero to twenty-one million dollars! What an incredible and FUN ride!

My new job required me to venture out into foreign countries to recruit new partners as a stranger on my own, no longer under the auspices of the big corporate boss. I was charged with not only securing distributors for my software company, but also convincing them to pay our company a six-figure cash advance! Once those distributors were on board, it was my responsibility to get them to produce significant sales results as independent operators I did not directly control.

*And we all had barriers to overcome: gender, age and, in my case, race. But I didn't worry or even think about any of that.*

It was a HUGE undertaking for anyone, much less a young Asian woman who had to deal with older, more experienced men from machismo cultures. I must have been quite naïve because it never occurred to me that I might be received differently because of my race, or that I might have to fight to be taken seriously because of my age or gender. I didn't expect it, prepare for it or worry about it. I just happily showed up in the foreign countries and did business in the way I knew how—playing my game of finding out what mattered to each person. Again, my keen desire to find out what others wanted out of life and their business helped me to forge strong relationships that garnered win-win partnerships. I now realize that my goal to make business dealings a fun playground for everyone involved was a key factor in my success.

We operate in a global market now, and the dotcom boom in the late 90s made twenty-year-old business geniuses a common sight. But in the 80s, as a success so young, I was a bit of an anomaly in the foreign markets. Why did the men from traditionally chauvinistic countries like Australia, Germany and Italy trust me enough to enter into multimillion dollar contracts with me and then wire-transfer hundreds of thousands of dollars to seal the partnership? Why did the middle-aged men from Asian countries like Japan and Korea treat me as their business equal? It wasn't that I was such a business genius, because I was not. I was hard working and reliable, but those attributes were not enough to transcend cultural barriers and open doors to major business deals.

I was naïve to these challenges at the time, but I realize now it was my innate sense of caring and collaboration that allowed me to gain the trust of my colleagues and sail past barriers that might have stopped others dead in their tracks. My cooperative approach to business made it possible for these men to get over their preconceived notions about race, women and youth.

When I played my game of trying to figure out what each player wanted, it was as if the best possible scenario for everyone came to me like magic.

When I asked in my own mind, "How can I help you to become the hero of your company now?" that is when the partnerships began. My colleagues felt at ease, inspired and cared for. Although I was not aware of the term "cooperative business" at the time, my natural instincts to operate in a different way brought me great success in the 1980s. I still wore the same colorful silk bow ties as all the other women climbing the proverbial corporate ladder, but my style was anything but status quo.

For example, I did not subscribe to the commonly held belief for negotiations that people should start out with certain negotiating "positions," where each player cooks up a strategy for getting the most out of the business deal. What a waste of time! All that posturing through multiple rounds of negotiations was so inefficient and absolutely no fun. Instead, I viewed each prospective business deal as an already-formed partnership. Together we worked openly to figure out what would make sense for everyone involved. To me, we were already playing as a team on the same side, not as adversaries jockeying for advantage, whether we ultimately reached that final handshake or not.

I came to see business in general as a game, too, but not a game of competition. For me, business was a game of passion and heart! I also looked at everyone as part of one giant puzzle, a total body, a unified whole. To disregard one puzzle piece would create an incomplete picture. Benefiting one party to the disadvantage of another was not the way I wanted to do business, and that came across to my associates.

---

*Again, my keen desire to find out what others wanted out of life and their business helped me to forge strong relationships that garnered win-win partnerships.*

---

My favorite little game became my greatest asset. As I put the puzzle together I would arrange the pieces to everyone's benefit. What are A's interests and what are his priorities now? What really matters to him? What can B bring to the table? What are C's passions and talents that could be further developed? And if D's experience and strengths do not fit well into this particular puzzle, then it is best that he become part of another game. I always cared a lot, but I was never a bleeding heart constant helper or had the need to win popularity contests with my business associates.

My focus was on how we could all take advantage of the new market opportunities and create a fun and lucrative playing field for all of us. How can we collaborate as a unified team with laser focus on achieving extraordinary results? The power of my vision and enthusiasm for the business potential in front of all of us quelled any misgivings many of the men I dealt with may have had.

I believe that as human beings we have an intuitive knowing that the world is a unified whole, so it is to our own benefit to work cooperatively and collaboratively for the good of everyone. But this tendency is taught out of us in favor of a focus on the individual, in favor of competition and separation. Yet when people follow their human tendency to help out because they genuinely care, it inspires those around them to get on board, reminding them of their own innate tendencies to serve the unified whole.

*For me, business was a game of passion and heart! I also looked at everyone as part of one giant puzzle, a total body, a unified whole.*

Operating from this deeper place of connection and unity can be difficult to describe but we can all feel it. Because I went deeper than the surface realities of age, gender and race, my colleagues forgot about them as well. Going deeper was not a conscious choice I made at the time. My focus was solely on my desire to find out what everyone wanted and then try to make sure he or she got it. And it worked beautifully.

I still play my little game of "What do you truly want and how can you go for it," much to my friends' amusement at times when they just want to sit back and relax. Today I am an entrepreneur forging my own path, and my game has become more than just a game. It has become a mission. And I LOVE what I do!

*Ruby Yeh is founder of Alive! Networks, a company that produces next generation books in an experiential, MULTI-MEDIA format. Her passion is to help visionary messengers increase their star power and catapult their powerful messages to the global market, while developing a lucrative electronic "info-preneur" business that empowers them to live a life of freedom, collaboration and fulfillment. www.aliveebooks.com.*

# Unite and Take Flight

DAVE AUSTIN

Standing before an audience of hundreds of eager students of cooperative business, I got that feeling — that feeling that you get when the plane is about to take off. Anticipation.

The moment just before the plane lifts off the ground is exciting, even for a seasoned traveler. It is a moment of anticipation about the flight, but also about the possibilities that await you at your destination. Though I had given countless speeches, I felt a similar thrill of anticipation. I had exciting news to share with the audience, and I knew that once I made the announcement, my "plane" would pick up speed, take off and fly. Life would never be the same.

"My theme today is the Three C's: Community, Cooperation and Collaboration," I began. "Now, more than ever, I am living my message." Being what you say is more important than what you say. We need to be the example of what we believe, what we teach, and most importantly, an example of the change we would like to see in the world. It was time for me to show people the power of community, cooperation and collaboration.

"Recently, I joined forces with Roger Anthony to create a powerful new program, 'Unite and Take Flight,'" I announced. The audience, which consisted of many people who also knew Roger and had experienced his transformational trainings, started bubbling with excitement. "I have a lot of great stories about cooperation, which is the message I give to the teams I have coached to victory. But to be living it in my own life is a tremendous gift."

Our joint venture took off from the moment we proclaimed it to the world. For years, I have coached my clients on the power of collaboration, but I had never experienced it so completely in my own endeavors.

We crystallized our vision very quickly, forming teams to put it into action. In uniting for a common goal we created a momentum that has been awe-inspiring.

*It's true; one and one do not make two — one and one united compounds to make five, seven, ten and eventually the exact number you need to realize your vision.*

The more we collaborate, the bigger our business grows. The more we focus on collaboration, the more opportunities show up to help us get the message out. It's the Law of Attraction at work: what you focus on multiplies. When two or more people focus on the same goal, the goal is not only achieved, *it expands*. In other words, you can experience the Law of Attraction on your own, but when you unite with others to create the same dream, the dream grows into something you could not even imagine individually. It's true; one and one do not make two — one and one united compounds to make five, seven, ten and eventually the exact number you need to realize your vision.

My collaboration with Roger began when I heard him speak about a year before we made the announcement. What he said resonated with me, so I introduced myself. We sat and talked for a while and realized we had a good rapport. We decided to stay in touch and to explore how we could help each other. I liked Roger and I was impressed by his approach to training and speaking. Roger's program has the highest retention rate in the world. Most people don't retain what they learn during workshops; the national average is thirteen percent. Roger's retention rate is over ninety percent! Working one-on-one with athletes, I have achieved a success rate of almost 100 percent. But working one-on-one is very different than speaking to a group for a few hours, or even a full day.

As we got to know each other, Roger and I realized that our combined talents and expertise would create an unbelievably powerful program, one that not only awakened people to their own limitless possibilities, but also enabled them to achieve and retain real change.

Collaboration isn't always easy. Roger and I were used to working solo. We had our own styles of communication and implementation, and we had to contend with our egos. Because of our individual successes, we each thought our way was, if not the *right* way, a *good* way to approach things. We were both right, but we had to come to an agreement and forge a new path together. Our partnership grew through talking to each other, learning to cooperate before we began collaborating. For our partnership to work, Roger and I had to be totally transparent with each other. We revealed our weaknesses and learned about each other's strengths. One of the bonuses of collaboration is the ability to recognize more of your own talents, as you see yourself through the eyes of your partner.

Our union became stronger when we let go of ego. Roger works differently than I do, so I've had to learn to give Roger a chance to *be Roger*. For example, I've learned that if I slow down and listen more, it takes the meeting to a new level, one that is deeper and more productive. I've also learned that it's pretty great to not have all of the pressure on me!

*We revealed our weaknesses and learned about each other's strengths. One of the bonuses of collaboration is the ability to recognize more of your own talents, as you see yourself through the eyes of your partner.*

Years ago, I played tennis on the pro circuit. I was always better in doubles than in singles. Other players thought I was just lucky because everyone I partnered with played better when he played with me. The truth was, it was the way we worked together that allowed *both* of us to be better tennis players.

One time I played with a guy who, after he hit the ball, would look at the crowd. He did it every time. I never played with him again because he wasn't cooperating. He was focused on himself and his image, rather than on winning the game as a team.

A team wins by trusting each other and by working together. When I work with sports teams I always emphasize that it is our cooperative spirit and collaboration at the highest level that will lead us to victory. It is not about the competition — the other team doesn't matter. When you focus on the other team, or the crowd or your own performance, you take yourself out of cooperation and change the course of events. You change the ending because now it's all about you, and you cannot accomplish on your own what a team can accomplish together. Working together takes everyone to new heights. When you unite, you take flight.

---

*We were meant to do this, to join together in a mission to help others unite and take flight.*

---

A few weeks after my announcement, Roger and I held our first "Unite and Take Flight" workshop, blending my freedom of expression with Roger's proven systems for retaining profound change. We used the concepts I created to help people become successful in the sports world and added Roger's systems to anchor the information. It was remarkable to tag team with Roger. It enabled participants to learn at a deeper level and to create results that are stronger and more powerful than we had been able to achieve working solo.

We know how to motivate people on our own, but it goes to a different level when we work together. Cooperating at the highest level gives us the freedom to play a better game, and to *enjoy* the journey of the game. We were meant to do this, to join together in a mission to help others unite and take flight.

There are no limits. I'm not talking about reaching your potential; I'm talking about flying higher than you ever thought possible. Your potential is limitless. When you work collaboratively, the sky is the limit. So unite and fly. Fly higher than you ever imagined. Set new records, exceed your own expectations. Soar.

Can you feel it? The anticipation? You're about to take off. Enjoy the ride!

*Affectionately known as the "Head" head coach, Dave Austin has an uncanny knack for bringing out the best in his clients. Building on degrees in both Psychology and Physical Education and on life experience, Dave developed specific methodology and results-oriented activities to help people take on greater challenges and produce breakthrough results. His performance coaching led to many individual and team successes, including the* L.A. *Dodgers rise from last place to winning the 2004 pennant.*

*An internationally renowned speaker and facilitator, Dave brings his inspired thought process and insights to countless audiences across the nation and as far away as Uzbekistan, sharing his success methods with not only professional and elite amateur athletes and teams, but also with entrepreneurs, corporate leaders, managers, sales professionals, corporate employees and educators.*

*A published author of several books including the critically acclaimed,* The Unfinished Cross – Listen to the Voice Within, *Dave's latest books are* Unite and Take Flight, *co-authored with Roger Anthony, and* Ordinary to Extraordinary: The 12 Steps to Exceeding Your Potential, *co-authored with his wife, Cathy Austin. To learn more about* Unite and Take Flight, *visit www.otherpeoplefirst.com. To learn more about Dave Austin, visit www.exceedpotential.com.*

# Teamwork Makes the Dream Work

SAJEELA CORMACK

All of us, no matter who we are, hold deep within ourselves the three essential keys to manifesting business attraction: Cooperation, Coherence and Collaboration.

We all know that the traditional business model is one of competition. I'm here to share with you that conducting business with a collaborative relationship model in mind is the new wave in the business world. It feels better, it runs smoother, and it harnesses energy that grows exponentially instead of fading away.

Thousands of businesses based on the old finite competitive model close their doors during challenging economic times, while ventures based on the cyclical system of sharing, cooperating, networking and giving back are thriving. Why? Because everyone wins within the cooperative model. It's that simple. When we are practicing with this awareness, we can't go on conducting business as if it were war. Nobody really wins at war, even the victors.

Over the past thirty-seven years, I have been involved in many different business ventures, as both an entrepreneur and investor. I have seen that, in order to fully participate in an environment of cooperation, coherence and collaboration, each of us must first develop qualities within ourselves that open the door for cooperative relationships at home *and* in business

Once upon a time, this idea was foreign to many in the business world. Nevertheless, top business gurus from many different cultures have known that it is essential to develop these important qualities, which I'm about to share with you. What makes human beings thrive also makes businesses thrive. Today, in true cooperative spirit, these secrets to success are being revealed so that everyone can benefit from their wisdom. We can all develop these qualities within ourselves — it's a matter of vision, choice, application and dedication. Collaboration embraces the practical wisdom we need to grow individually. As a social species, we need that information in order to take the next step — co-operating in making a better world.

In 2001, I was introduced to a gentleman who was looking for investors. Listening carefully to his presentation, I decided to take a new approach to business investing: I would look at the character at the helm at least as closely as the information he was presenting. The investment would be in him, not just his business. So I asked him a lot of questions, including many personal ones. What did he value, most? What drove him? Was he a team player? Did he honor his word? Did he demonstrate leadership skills that proved a benefit to the team and delivered the end goal? Was he an open communicator? How could I be sure?

As I began to unravel the character of this young man (whom we'll call Jack), I found that he was solid, admirable and trustworthy. A picture unfolded before me, a vision of the bright and abundant future of his company. Even though others whom I trusted had a negative view of Jack's project, I decided to trust my intuition and take the business opportunity that he offered me.

*Collaboration embraces the practical wisdom we need to grow individually. As a social species, we need that information in order to take the next step—cooperating in making a better world.*

Thank heavens I did! I invested five-hundred thousand dollars — at the time, a sizeable amount for me — in a company that was then worth less than one million dollars. Today, the short forecast for the company is for growth to five-hundred million. And a shareholding in four other businesses of similar magnitude has also transpired from this first venture.

Vital qualities a great collaborator must possess are vision and attention to detail. Visionaries see the big picture, the long-term view; they use their intuition, creativity and innovative ideas to guide them along paths where others might fear to tread. Attention to detail enables foresight of potential challenges to show us innovative possibilities. We need the wide angle *and* the close view. A collaborator must also be self-aware and self-loving enough to listen to her intuition and let it guide her in both ways of seeing.

Once we commit to our vision, we must believe in, trust in and have faith in that vision. We need to feed it with our passion, optimism and enthusiasm. These gifts are contagious. Take Jack and me, for example. Over the years, when he has thought small, I've thought big. When Jack first approached me, he spoke of selling his company for a million dollars the following year. Spurred by my vision, I asked, many times, "Do you realize what you've got here? What about a *billion* in *several* years?" Together, we grew from under a million to three, to five, to twelve, to twenty-eight, to our current potential of five-hundred million dollars.

Because we have embarked upon a path of collaboration, Jack and I don't have the standard business owner/investor relationship. Instead of just sending me stacks of financials, he asks for my perspective on issues and my appraisal of documents. I feel he values my input, ideas, vision, mentorship, support and enthusiasm for our project. This has broadened his horizons. Similarly, I too have enjoyed great personal and professional growth as a result of our cooperative relationship. Asking more proactive, penetrating questions of Jack right from the beginning established a wonderfully clear and open dynamic between us. The success of our communication is also due in part to my study, practice and teaching of the NLP (neuro-linguistic programming) Emotional Resilience and Open Communication Model.

It is vital that as collaborators, we become open communicators, making our strongest efforts to be clear and succinct in our words and intentions. Great communicators are also active listeners who embrace the individual qualities of each team member. True listeners are team players who perform and delegate tasks according to ability, not hierarchy. This makes communication and management so much easier. Great collaborators don't have to lose time in negotiations that go nowhere. Nor do they engage in power plays that feed their own egos. There is trust and co-operation.

*Once we commit to our vision, we must believe in, trust in and have faith in that vision. We need to feed it with our passion, optimism and enthusiasm. These gifts are contagious.*

When the why is big enough, the how becomes easy. With all team members exercising their greatest abilities in pursuit of the common goal, while taking personal responsibility for their own important pieces of the puzzle, coherence naturally emerges within a venture. Great collaborators are secure in themselves and emotionally resilient enough to allow for others to step into their own greatness and empowerment. They are also lifelong learners, with a fearless passion for original thinking. If, for example, I had been consumed by fear and unwilling to think outside my box, I would have emotionally blocked myself from seeing the great potential in Jack's company. Many people view startups as risky. But take it from me, investing in a startup that functions cooperatively is a much more positive choice than investing in a competitive business of any kind. We are here to help each other. If we look at each other in the right way, we see that all of our skills are complementary.

As a nutritionist, I had a great idea for a children's book about the acid-alkaline connection, and how knowing the pH of a child's blood could fight her obesity, give her more energy and even potentially save her life. In search of an illustrator for the book, I met with a cartoonist.

While we talked about nutrition in the context of the book project, the cartoonist shared with me that he wanted to release some weight; that his relationship with his wife wasn't in a good place; and that his business needed help. He was feeling fatigued and overwhelmed. So as he worked on bringing life to the characters in my book, I helped him bring his own existence back to life through my own nutrition and energy work. We looked at everything: his diet (foods to implement, foods to avoid); his lifestyle; how he communicated with his wife and his colleagues. I told him that with greater energy, he would attract more business. I also suggested that he bring color into his home and work environments and that he start to wear more color to increase vibrational energy. "We need to fill your cup so that it is always overflowing — so you don't come from a place of lack and give out the underlying message of neediness. You need to convey abundance."

*We are here to help each other. If we look at each other in the right way, we see that all of our skills are complementary.*

The cartoonist changed not just his diet, but his lifestyle; he started wearing color, painted his office and began playing music in the workplace. Within one week, he'd released seven kilos and had a better relationship with his wife. His work turned around too. Full of energy and possibility, the cartoonist attracted two great new employees and three big new projects. While we worked together, the flow of energy continued. It flowed both ways. With my help, the cartoonist turned his life around; with his help, my treasured children's book became a reality. Neither of us could have done without the help of the other. Then came the word-of-mouth referrals.

Collaboration is one of the universal laws. It manifests great rewards for everyone involved. Tenacity, positivity and determination led Jack's business, and the cartoonist's world, to grow like beautiful gardens of many hues and colors. Thanks to the wonderful communities created, they both continue to cultivate — givers, sharers, networkers, staff and investors who possess great talents as collaborators — and they are poised to keep on flourishing.

When you consider your dreams, ask yourself: How do I need to develop myself as a collaborator? Then, take it a step further and ask: How can I make this product or business a tool for collaboration? Commit to your own evolution. Trust yourself and the strength of your vision. Practice speaking and listening with passion and intuition and you will effortlessly call forth your very own cooperative community.

*Based in Australia, Sajeela Cormack has been a nutritionist and personal development coach for over thirty years. Through her practices of massage, natural healing, positive psychology, wealth creation and spiritual growth, she has healed herself of crippling arthritis and life-threatening injuries.*

*Sajeela was the first to bring Ayurvedic infant massage to Australia, where it has grown to become a movement. She has studied with some of the world's most respected teachers, including Anthony Robbins, Deepak Chopra, Brian Tracy, Wayne Dyer, James Rhone and Louise Hay. Sajeela loves to assist others to remember who they innately are, discover their purpose, communicate openly and access their highest potential. She is also the author of* Energy, Enthusiasm, Excellence, *and a co-author of* Ageless Vitality.

# Party Your Way to Success

SYNDI SEID

One morning, just two years after launching my international etiquette business, I received a phone call that changed my life.

"We would like you to appear on ABC Television Network's *Good Morning, America* with Charlie Gibson," the producer said. "Do you have time for a few questions?"

*Good Morning, America*? I was stunned. I had no media experience. None. Not even one back page article in my local newspaper. Talk about trial by fire! Somehow, I made it through the interview process, wondering all the while why they had picked little old me to appear on the show. The producer informed me that Charlie Gibson had interviewed an Italian cookbook author the week before. During this segment, he had spilled spaghetti all over his chin. This gave the show's producers the idea for a follow-up interview; they wanted an etiquette expert to teach Charlie how to properly eat spaghetti and other hard-to-eat foods.

"You're great. We'd like you to come on Monday," the producer declared. It was Friday. Before she hung up I just had to ask...

"Is there a reason why you want a nobody like me?" I didn't want to sound unprofessional, but the opportunity seemed to come out of nowhere and I was slightly confused... flattered, but confused.

"We just thought we'd have somebody new," she replied. "Gwen Mazer recommended you."

Ah, my new friend Gwen. Mystery solved. When I met Gwen at the National Association of Women Business Owners, we had become fast friends. The producers at *Good Morning, America* had called Gwen, an image consultant who had regularly made television appearances, to book her on the show. She informed them she was not an etiquette expert, but knew someone who was and would be perfect for the segment: her friend, Syndi Seid.

Friend. I can't tell you how many connections I've made through friends, or how many people I have helped because they are my friends. When you seek to develop friendships with people, rather than network in order to get more business, you end up with more business than you can handle. More importantly, your circle of friends — colleagues, clients and potential clients — is cooperative, loyal and sincere. People do business with people they know, like and trust. Given the choice between doing business with a vendor you consider a friend or a vendor with whom you have little rapport, which vendor will you choose?

This concept goes beyond networking, which has become a tool to generate new leads rather than form relationships. Building "friendships" with the intent to generate new business is insincere, and no fun for anyone involved. Which is why I don't network. I party. I love to party. I love giving parties and going to parties. I love parties so much, that when I launched my business, I knew parties would be an integral part of my professional life. Meeting people, socializing, having fun together — these are the things I enjoy most in life.

*Your circle of friends — colleagues, clients and potential clients — is cooperative, loyal and sincere.*

My love of parties inspired me to come up with three main components my company had to have: first, it had to be a pursuit that naturally combined both business and pleasure. It had to be fun, something that would continuously evolve. And, it had to be helpful, touching people's lives in a positive way.

Over the past sixteen years I have been able to meet those three original requirements I set for myself in business, due in large part to my approach to partying. I jump at the chance to meet new people and have fun, and I always focus on creating new relationships with absolutely *no ulterior motive.*

Partying definitely has its perks. Not only do I combine business with pleasure, I have discovered that partying is the perfect way to date my husband! I could be working 24–7 and never see him, but because we attend and host social gatherings together, we get to spend time having fun on a regular basis. But the best perk of all is getting to know people, and nurturing and building friendships.

Author and former White House Etiquette Expert Marjabelle Young Stewart once said, "*When you want to get your point across, entertain!*" I believe in that statement. I've seen it in action time after time.

*Inviting clients into my home and my circle of friends lets them know I appreciate their business and I appreciate them.*

Before we downsized our house, my husband and I hosted an annual midsummer salmon fishing party, a blowout for over a hundred guests. The Friday before the party, twenty-five people would head past the Golden Gate Bridge to fish for salmon. Then, on Saturday, they would come to our house with their family and friends and we would all have a blast cooking and eating the catch — and drinking great wine, another love we all share.

From the beginning of my business, I invited clients to our salmon party. When I hosted a client it was a special thing; it meant that person was someone with whom I wanted to become closer friends. Our party solidified relationships with my clients and built customer relations based on warmth and trust.

Inviting clients into my home and my circle of friends lets them know I appreciate their business and I appreciate them. Did I get new or more business from my once-a-year salmon bash? Sure I did, and so did many of my guests. When people are genuinely enjoying each other with only one goal — to have fun — connections are meaningful, genuine and happen organically. People like to do business with fun people.

Over the years, most of my clients have become my friends. Once *your* clients become your friends, they will always think of you first in business. In fact, they will actually *dismiss* potential new inquiries, simply because they would rather work with you, their friend.

Inviting clients to social events throughout the year allows them to see me in a different environment. They get to know a more informal, intimate side of me. And, they meet and make connections with my other friends, who serve as good advocates for me and for my business without even trying. Partying with clients allows clients to see you as a whole person.

When you mix friends with clients in social situations, you show your clients who you really are. Combining business and pleasure gives your clients and prospects the opportunity to truly get to know you.

Your clients will always remember the great times they've had with you socially and associate you with fun, friendship and positive experiences. And, they may even think of you when an exciting prospect turns up, one for which you would be perfect.

Gwen and I were not old buddies and we were not regular networking acquaintances. We were friends, new friends, who fostered an authentic relationship based on mutual interest. Gwen knew the real me, and because she considered me a friend, she gladly sent an amazing opportunity my way.

Because Gwen recommended me to the producers at *Good Morning, America*, I received national exposure within my first two years of business. And after that memorable Monday morning, when I taught Charlie Gibson proper table manners, my business really took off. I was able to "hang my shingle" on that experience, attracting new clients... and friends.

When people know, like and trust you, they become champions for you and your business. They want you to succeed. They happily refer you to new clients and opportunities with no thought for how they may benefit themselves. Just as any good friend would.

*Syndi Seid is the etiquette expert of choice for the world's leading organizations and in the media, offering comprehensive training on social etiquette and international business protocol. As founder of Advanced Etiquette Worldwide, Syndi helps senior executives, business professionals and main-line employees overcome their fears and insecurities to find poise, confidence and authority in any situation, anywhere in the world.*

*As a recognized, leading world's expert on business protocol and etiquette, Syndi Seid has served numerous corporate giants, including Hewlett-Packard Worldwide, Sprint International and the Miss Universe Pageant. Her media credits include appearing on* ABC*'s* Good Morning, America, *CBS's* Eye on America, *Fox's* Trading Spouses, *HGTV's* Party At Home, *and Discovery Channel's* Picture This.

*Syndi is the etiquette expert for staples.com and a contributing writer for SBTV.com. You can also find her video tips on www.bnet.com and www.you-tube .com. Her etiquette information appears in a nationally distributed column in* AsianWeek. *She is a contributor to the book* Business Etiquette for Dummies, *and her own book,* Etiquette In Minutes: 201 Practical Tips For Business and Social Behavior From an International Etiquette Expert, *is now available at www.etiquetteinminutes.com. To learn more about Syndi, visit www.advancedetiquette.com.*

# Embrace Your Competition

GIL ORTEGA

Driving through the sweltering Nevada desert, my entire life packed into my car, I prayed for air conditioning — and a fresh start. Days away from a new year, I pointed my car toward Las Vegas, toward the year 2001 and toward a blow-up mattress with my name on it. In just two years, my entire life had changed dramatically. Having invested the money from the sale of my successful lead-generation business in a promising Internet start-up, I had gone from being a financially independent entrepreneur to a casualty of the dotcom meltdown.

When the dotcom boom bottomed out, it left plenty of people just like me: sleeping on air beds, couches and in their parents' basements, trying to recover from the shock and disappointment and figure out what to do next. Fortunately, I knew how to start something amazing from scratch. Maybe it's my love for business, or maybe it's my hopeful artist's soul, but even after I lost all of my money, somehow I knew that I would recover. After all, I knew a little something about how to spot opportunities.

---

*Opportunities for collaboration are everywhere, and if you pay attention, you will spot them. When you are able to connect individuals, groups, teams or businesses together for mutual gain, success is inevitable.*

---

At fifteen I started my first business, Chili Productions, promoting concerts and nightclub events. I've always been an artist with an entrepreneurial aptitude, and my business satisfied my two passions. Rather than pay through the nose for the usual venues, I came up with a way to obtain unique places to hold my events. I approached restaurant owners, asking if I could turn their dining spaces into nightclubs after 10:00 PM. "I'll pay you rent for one night, and you can keep your bartender on and increase your bar revenue substantially," I explained. The collaboration was a win-win: I was able to secure exclusive rights to cool locations at a fraction of the rental fees that traditional venues charged, and the restaurants cleaned up on bar bills.

The music business welcomes new ideas, so it wasn't long before I was a real music impresario. Working with record companies, managing bands, transforming venues into exciting environments. It was an amazing time, and I loved every minute of it.

Opportunities for collaboration are everywhere, and if you pay attention, you will spot them. When you are able to connect individuals, groups, teams or businesses for mutual gain, success is inevitable. As a young entrepreneur I wasn't consciously applying this collaborative strategy, I simply enjoyed making things happen. In 1995 I started my first lead-generation business, which operated entirely offline. It took off, and in a few short years I sold the company in search of new adventures. The results weren't exactly what I had in mind; it was a more harrowing than exciting time. And instead of the big payoff, I ended up with nothing but my car and a few possessions.

It took two months, but I finally made it out of my funk — and my friend's one-bedroom apartment. I spent the better part of 2001 working for a travel-related list company, only to be shut down again after the 9/11 tragedy stalled the travel industry.

One day I was introduced to someone who was generating leads online. Lead generation had brought me great success and financial reward, but I had no idea how to do it through the Internet. So I asked him how he did it, and once I was sure I had a good source for quality leads, I set up shop.

I started my second lead-generation business with fifty dollars, a basic website template and a phone. My main goal was to make enough money to pay the phone bill every month. Within one year we broke $1,300,000 in revenue.

Again, the success of my new business was built on spotting an opportunity to collaborate. This time, my collaborators were also my competition. The lead-generation business is highly competitive. Everyone is clamoring for customers, and also desperate to find quality leads to deliver to them. In my online research I discovered a problem that every single lead business had: either they had too many leads, or too few. It sounds like an obvious opportunity for any go-getter; however, due to the competitiveness of the lead companies, they didn't see it.

Most people think of leads as lists of contacts, but leads are actually real-time responses to advertising. My competitors had clients who needed to buy only very specific types of leads — I knew that because I had my own clients' orders to fill. In my research, I noted lead companies with large inventories of one type of lead, and competitors looking for similar leads. These companies could be very useful to each other, but because they were "in competition" with each other, no one even considered working together to get what they needed. Rather than jump into the vast pool of lead generators vying for leads and customers, I decided to become a wholesaler, selling leads to other lead companies who were, essentially, my competition.

It started with a simple phone call. "I have a good lead source, and I'll give you leads at almost my cost to help fill your lead flow," I offered. "In return, are you able to produce more of the leads you have?"

Everyone I called was suspicious at first. Why not? I was after the same clients they were after; they were right to be wary of my offer. Still, when a deal is done right, in good faith, and you perform, it works out.

Once my competitors took off their "suspicious glasses" and recognized me as someone who could help them, I began connecting all of the lead companies. I came to them and said, "Look, let me grow your company and your lead flow for you." And so I began building relationships with my competitors. Selling them leads was easy because I was in the same boat with them.

When you embrace your competitors as collaborators, you not only solve major problems in your industry, you create tremendous income-generating opportunities for everyone involved. When we got over the initial hurdle of mistrust, I was the person they wanted to buy from. Not in spite of the fact that I was their competitor, but *because I was their competitor.* I understood the business, which provided me with a huge advantage. Soon I became the main hub exchange for leads, the go-to matchmaker in the industry. Because I had a consortium of lead companies, I had the buying power to purchase leads at volume prices, and to demand better contracts.

*When you embrace your competitors as collaborators, you not only solve major problems in your industry, you create tremendous income-generating opportunities for everyone involved.*

The matching process was about finding connections. When you are open to collaboration, you are better able to spot the key connections that will take your business to the next level. My buying power allowed me to generate enough lead flow to funnel into my own retail lead-generation business. Because I was collaborating with other businesses, I was able to significantly grow both sides of my business at a rapid rate. And because I established a minimum order, my clients began collaborating with each other, forming co-ops so that they could order from me. The co-ops were made up of related businesses, some of which were directly competing with one another. Yet in working cooperatively, they all benefited because they were able to order quality leads from my company.

When I look back on my life so far, I see a pattern, a common denominator in all of my wins: collaboration. All of my best ideas were born in that spirit. From my days in the music business to my work in the lead and advertising industries, collaboration has always been "standard operating procedure."

Even in my work as a painter I create collaboratively, while other artists are very often solitary. Dissatisfied with the traditional applications of paint to canvas, I developed a technique that enables my subjects to participate in creating their own portraits, using imprints of their own bodies. It's not just about what I want to create, but also what my models want to get from the experience, and from the end result.

Cooperative business is about being open to all of the possibilities of collaboration, and in that openness, attracting genius ideas, essential partners and perfect timing. It is beyond business — it is the art of business.

No matter your circumstance — whether you're sleeping on a blow-up mattress or a king-sized bed — extraordinary opportunities will come your way when you seek to connect with others for mutual gain, for the sheer joy of it and for the good of the planet.

*Awarded the prestigious Entrepreneur of the Year from the San Diego County Hispanic Chamber of Commerce (SDCHCC) in 2007, Gil Ortega started his first business — Chili Productions — at the age of fifteen. Marrying Gil's artistic and entrepreneurial talents, over the next ten years Chili Productions would become one of the top event and production companies in Southern California.*

*The founder of several successful lead-generation businesses, Gil founded Leads to Wealth, Inc. with only fifty dollars and grew the company to over twelve million dollars in sales in four years. His latest business, an innovative advertising network, is set to launch in 2009. An accomplished artist creating under the name Rick Bliss, Gil developed a painting technique that enables the human body to be an active participant in the genesis of art. To learn more about Gil, visit www.gilortega.net and www.rickbliss.com.*

# United:
# Building One Dream at a Time

LORIE A. L. NICHOLAS, PH.D.

I must have made a thousand calls. Each time I spoke with someone, I held the phone so tightly that not even the sweat on my palms loosened my grip. Some of the voices on the other end were high-pitched, some low. Some were smooth, and some were rough, like a smoker's.

But no matter the timbre or tone, whenever the representatives I had been speaking to came back after making me wait for a few moments, their answer was always the same. It was as if they were all reading from the same script, tailored specifically to me: "I'm sorry, but we're unable to help you. Your credit scores are too low and your debt-to-income ratio is way too high." It was particularly appalling that almost all of them spoke with the same sort of fake sympathy, as if they really *were* sorry. Maybe they were. And maybe they were sorry because they were tired of telling people what they'd just told me. They'd been saying the same words to so many people.

I was one of millions of victims of the subprime mortgage disaster. The people who kept saying "no" to me were representatives of the banks and mortgage companies I kept appealing to for help. I had to overcome my disappointment to realize that these people saying "no" didn't have as much to do with me as it did with the terrible situation the country, and the world, had plunged into.

You can never find solutions to your problems if you perceive yourself as a victim, because making yourself a victim robs you of any empowerment. And when you deprive yourself of empowerment, you end up placing the power and possibility of solutions into someone else's hands. Victim though I was, I certainly had a part in my housing woes. I had been a renter for most of my life, but after hearing so many real estate gurus argue that home ownership was the better way to go, I decided to test my skills at real estate. After all, I was finally establishing myself in my career, and if I was going to keep forking over money every month for a roof over my head, why not do so towards an investment?

I've always been a do-it-yourself kind of person, so I attended several real estate classes to learn the terminology, and eventually pursued and purchased my first home, a condo in New York. My mortgage broker explained various options for financing. The one I took had a fixed rate for the first three years, with an adjustable rate after that. I liked it because of the low payments. "Now, during the adjustable period, those interest rates can go up," my broker said. No problem, I thought. Unfortunately, I was still thinking like a renter. When he said they could go up, I thought he meant in the same way rents could go up: twenty, maybe fifty dollars a month. That was my naïveté, and that was my mistake. I signed on the dotted line, and eventually those rates rose much higher than I ever imagined.

---

*You can never begin to access a solution until you first frankly admit, to yourself and possibly others, where you've made mistakes. And to not admit your own mistakes is to again assume the helpless role of victim.*

---

You know the rest of the story. I could not get anyone to help me refinance my mortgage loan. Everyone said I was too high a risk. Even government programs set up to help us mortgage crisis casualties told me I was too high-risk to help. I was feeling lower than low. I could not believe that so much that I'd worked for over the years was going to be lost because of one mistake. You can never begin to access a solution until you first frankly admit, to yourself and possibly others, where you've made mistakes. And to not admit your own mistakes is to again assume the helpless role of victim.

I started to seek alternative solutions, and was diligent about it. Then, one day, at a professional business meeting, I met Teresa Martin, a real estate and foreclosure defense and credit restoration attorney. When I discovered her profession, I told her about some of my problems. And finally, finally, I got some guidance towards alternative solutions. We won't always reach solutions to problems when we want them, but if we are diligent, answers will eventually come, and often when and where we least expect them. That's why it is always important to keep an open mind and, more significantly, an open spirit: nothing can enter something that is closed.

Teresa gave me sound advice. She offered suggestions, helping me strategize various options I could pursue, and even helped me prepare everything in case I did need to foreclose. Eventually, I did sell my property because it was the smartest approach to take. But when I sold it, I did so knowing exactly what I was doing and why. More importantly, though, as I worked with Attorney Martin, she introduced me to Al Johnson.

---

*We won't always reach solutions to problems when we want them, but if we are diligent, answers will eventually come, and often when and where we least expect them.*

---

Al Johnson heads up two real estate investment organizations that have monthly meetings. At these meetings, people get great advice from Al about their real estate projects. If you want to buy, Al teaches you how to calculate expenses to make sure you can afford what you're getting, and he makes sure you add room for incidental expenses. If I had had his expertise the first time around, I wouldn't have made the mistakes I'd made. I wouldn't have put myself at that point where I said, "I can JUST afford this." Al did something even better for me than giving me great real estate advice. He introduced me to my mentor, Marc Grant. At his monthly meetings, Al often had guest speakers come talk to the group. Two of them were Marc and his wife, Rhonda, founders of The Success Connection Team Corp., and authors of the forthcoming book *Pursuing Your Freedom: How to Break Through in Every Area of Your Life.*

Marc came to the group to conduct a workshop for people interested in establishing a business. He blew me away. He was, and is, the most professional person I've ever met — eloquent, attentive, competent, astute. And his story spoke to me. Marc came from a background of bankruptcy, losing several businesses along his bumpy path. And yet, he was still able to emerge from the ashes not only with a successful business but with a strong desire to help others succeed. That mattered to me. I have a Ph.D., in Clinical-Community Psychology. I chose my profession because I was always interested in helping others.

When I was trying to figure out what business I wanted to establish, my desire to help others remained at the forefront. However, when I was dealing with my real estate woes, I was thinking only of me. That's when Marc told me what are perhaps the most important words I've ever heard: "Look within, Lorie. The solution to your problems is directly in front of you."

I don't know why those words mattered, but when Marc said them, something clicked. I recalled the personal financial challenges I was seeking relief from, as well as the daily mental and physical challenges I encountered. I also thought about all the resources and support I was now connected to, and how those strengthened and empowered me. In an instant, the vision for Dream Builders United became crystal clear. You have to trust the process of achieving your dream. It only seemed as if my idea for Dream Builders United came in a flash, but I'd actually been working toward it for years. I didn't know I was working toward it, and I didn't need to know. I only needed to trust the process and stay on the path.

I created Dream Builders United to help people learn how to help themselves. Too many people around me were losing their homes partly because they weren't financially literate. But it wasn't just that. I wanted to create a cooperative that not only helped people with their current housing concerns, but also provided them with resources and support they could use for the rest of their lives. I wanted to help individuals and families overcome the odds stacked against them by teaching them how to strategize, and to solve their own problems, without being dependent upon systems or people that don't have their best interests at heart.

The reason the old sayings stick around so long is that they never lose their truth. That certainly applies to this adage, which embodied my thinking as I created Dream Builders United: Give a person a fish, he eats for one day; teach him how to fish, he eats for a lifetime.

I recruited all the people who were part of my path to be a part of Dream Builders United. I'm the CEO, and we have Teresa Martin for legal advice, Al Johnson for real estate advice and Marc, my mentor, to help people establish a business and do their taxes correctly. Dream Builders United is also equipped with resources to meet many other financial needs. Also on our team is William Moore, an Ambassador of a credit restoration program. He provides expertise to connect people to a service that can help them get their credit reviewed and, if possible, rehabilitated.

*I only needed to trust the process and stay on the path.*

Through the Law of Attraction, the people who offered the resources I needed during my time of turmoil became my cooperative business partners. Like attracts like, and you will attract into your life whatever you focus on. We literally attract the things, people, ideas and circumstances that resonate at the same energy frequencies as our own.

Working together, all of us at Dream Builders United can target and help more families through the strength of our combined services.

In addition, we are building a foundational supportive network of individuals, in which one homeowner reaches out to help another potential, or at-risk, homeowner.

As we help people become Builders of their Dreams, toward a legacy of financial freedom, we are part of something uniquely, genuinely special.

*Lorie A. L. Nicholas is the CEO of Dream Builders United, an organization geared toward educating and empowering families around financial literacy and building a legacy of financial freedom. She holds a doctorate in Clinical-Community Psychology and is a staff psychologist at the Federal Bureau of Prisons. She also serves as an adjunct professor in the Department of Law, Police Science and Criminal Justice Administration as well as the Department of Psychology at John Jay College of Criminal Justice (CUNY).*

*Lorie is a successful motivational speaker, real estate investor, entrepreneur and author; she has presented at many conferences and conducted many workshops and trainings on stress management, race relations, the criminal justice system, substance abuse and violence. She is available for speaking engagements and trainings and can be reached at info@dreambuildersunited.com.*

# The Missing Link

LAUREN SOLOMON

"May I ask you a question? What do you think of my shirt?" Bill asked.

I looked up from my tray to see Bill, a finance expert and speaker whom I had met earlier that day. Amidst all the entrepreneurs dressed in business or business casual attire, Bill's Hawaiian shirt stood out like a neon sign. I smiled.

"Why?" I asked. In my work as an image consultant, it is common for people to ask me about their appearance. Though Bill seemed to genuinely want my opinion, I could sense a subtle note of challenge in the question. Bill had never before heard of an image consultant who worked with "real people." He thought the only people who needed professional help with their images were celebrities and politicians.

"People compliment me on it. I think my shirt has become a signature for me," he added.

I am committed to empowering people in reaching their full potential by creating an image that reflects their aspirations. So, I had come to this conference — where I met Bill — seeking opportunities to help propel small businesses and business owners to new heights through the power of their presented images. My goal was to attract four people or projects that touched my heart and were truly ready, with the support of my coaching, to step through the door to a new level of success — a level beyond anything they had ever imagined on their own.

"Does your shirt tell me something about your business or expertise?" I asked.

"No. Why?" Bill replied.

"Because in my world, the clothes you wear carry a powerful message. That particular style of shirt tells me that you either live in Hawaii or that you are probably retired and living a casual, resort-style life," I explained. "How does your shirt help people learn anything about you or your experience? How does it represent your business? Are people actually complimenting you on your shirt, or are they *commenting* on it?"

"Good questions." Bill smiled. We parted ways.

Deeply inspired by their creative projects or new ventures, creators are frequently under the mistaken belief that the world will immediately embrace and invest in their visions — overlooking the real importance of aligning the power of personal image with the strength of creativity. Brilliant people looking for investors or partners recognize the power of personal image to ensure a profound confidence. They know that they cannot rely on their talent and genius alone. Their images must project a willingness to be the CEOs of their own success. An empowered, polished and well-defined image is the missing link between the wish and the manifestation.

*An empowered, polished and well-defined image is the missing link between the wish and the manifestation.*

The day after our conversation about the shirt, I found Bill once again in the food line. Gone was the Hawaiian shirt, replaced with a dapper business suit, dress shirt and tie. "I've been looking for you all day," he said excitedly. "What do you think of my look now?"

Over lunch, I explained to Bill that I could see he was someone who took great pride in his appearance and invested in a fine wardrobe. However, even in his business best, his image was that of a kindly grandfather, not that of someone who was providing cutting-edge business strategies to corporations and entrepreneurs.

"It's not just about the clothes," I explained. "It's about connecting with a place deep inside and then determining how you want to feel about yourself, and how you want others to receive and respond to you."

When you look in the mirror and feel excited, when you know you are presenting your very best self, you attract exciting people and opportunities. Things were starting to make sense to Bill. He could see that he needed to cultivate an image that reflected his skills, his experience and his goals. I started asking more questions. Was he attracting the clients he really wanted? Who would he like as prospects? Where would he like to take his business in the future?

As we talked, I learned more about Bill's story and realized I had found someone who was ready to take himself to a new level. I knew that our work together would yield remarkable results, and quickly. Within six months, Bill's business close ratio improved significantly, he was attracting more appropriate clients and he saw a twenty-five percent increase in revenue.

Unexpectedly, somewhere between his closet and the eyeglass store, Bill started asking me questions about my business. He was intent on showing me that I was an ideal client prospect for him, and that his new image *did* reflect his ability to strategize my business in a new and powerful way. After my first strategy session with Bill, I gained a clearer picture of the vision I held for my own business. In addition to helping me strategize my business, Bill has brought me in to work with some of his clients. And, the opportunity to offer Bill as an ally to my existing clients has been greatly beneficial. Bill and I have helped each other tremendously, and have partnered on numerous projects to grow our businesses, our client bases and our financial abundance.

---

*When you look in the mirror and feel excited, when you know you are presenting your very best self, you attract exciting people and opportunities.*

---

The same week I met Bill, I discovered numerous extraordinary individuals doing amazing work on projects that interested me. And, in less than one year, I began working with two-dozen new client-companies, all of which have since moved forward dramatically. At the same time, I have received valuable counsel from experts who have generously supported me in my business strategy, growth and marketing. I now have a dedicated team of people to call upon.

Meeting Bill — and so many others who are living examples of success through the cooperative business model — has shown me yet another layer of our own ability to create and attract the lives we wish to live. When you focus solely on giving, you relax and allow good things to come your way. Shifting your focus in this way empowers you, opens you up and enables you to attract opportunities that lead to your optimum success.

*At the same time, I have received valuable counsel from experts who have generously supported me in my business strategy, growth and marketing. I now have a dedicated team of people to call upon.*

My own experience of opening up through giving showed me something profound. I learned that, in the same way that creating a dynamic, authentic image is the missing link between hoping for success and achieving it, working *cooperatively* was my missing link. And it has attracted more fun, new friends and greater levels of success than I have ever experienced before. When you show up as your very best self, you are able to give generously and are open to receive. All things are possible.

*Lauren Solomon, MBA, AICI, CIP, is the trusted image advisor to CEOs, millionaires and business start-ups alike. President of LS Image Associates in New York City and author of* Image Matters! First Steps on the Journey to Your Best Self, *she is the former Vice President of Professional Image Development at Chase Manhattan Bank; creator and lead instructor of the professional skills workshop,* The Brand Called Me, *at the New York University Stern School of Business; a faculty member of the Image Consulting Certification Program at the Fashion Institute of Technology; and President Emeritus of the Association of Image Consultants International (AICI). Lauren is the Career TV image expert and an image industry spokesperson. She has been featured on Lifetime Television, MSNBC, CNN-fn,* WOR Radio *and* Voice America Women. *She has also appeared in* The New York Times, New York, Men's Health *and other publications.*

# The "Real" Great Motivator

HARRY P. LAY

When I first heard about the revolutionary concept of working collaboratively with other businesses rather than competing against them, I was skeptical. It challenged my whole paradigm about how to lead and run a successful business. But, once I embraced it, the cooperative business model brought me greater success than I ever dreamed possible.

As a former athlete, I once believed that the thing that got people out of bed every morning — and inspired them to aim higher, work harder, run faster and stay longer than the other guys — was the desire to win.

So, when I started out in business in 1969, I naturally believed that competition within and between companies was the great motivator. It seemed only natural to apply the principles I had learned in sports to my career as a Certified Public Accountant (CPA), a corporate executive and a trusted advisor. Competing against the guy down the hall for the same coveted promotion was the norm. Battling against other firms for high-profile clients was simply standard operating procedure. Like most people, the competitive strategy was what I knew. I would eventually discover there was a better way to motivate people — and I would learn it the hard way.

By 1988, I had been a partner in a CPA firm for over ten years. All was well. If I didn't stub my toe, my career was set. Still, I knew there was more in store for me. I wanted a challenge. When the opportunity arose to take over as Chief Financial Officer (CFO) — and ultimately President — of an architectural and engineering firm, I took a risk and accepted the offer. During our first strategic planning retreat, I learned that the firm's owners wanted me to help them increase their individual earnings from less than fifty thousand to one million dollars per year, in the span of ten years. I'm all for dreaming big, but that was quite a leap!

After researching pay scales, I learned that architects were on the bottom of the professional services' compensation ladder. When I finally put pencil to paper and realized the enormity of this challenge, I thought, what have I done? The goal seemed totally unattainable. Then I thought, who am I to tell them no? I knew they were motivated and would do anything to reach their goal. So I took it on.

---

*Like most people, the competitive strategy was what I knew. I would eventually discover there was a better way to motivate people — and I would learn it the hard way.*

---

The firm eventually attracted and retained a number of large corporate clients in the retail, restaurant and hospitality industries. We were doing "okay." We were growing and staying busy, but still not producing the desired profits. So we decided to divide our employees into seven teams, segregated by client. The key to our competitive strategy was a profit-sharing bonus plan that awarded the teams with the highest profits. If a client team produced no profits, it earned no bonus.

We continually published the results of each team's profits, hoping that this would motivate the "losing" teams. But our strategy backfired in a big way. Some of the client teams produced profits, and some did not. Neither result was necessarily due to the team itself. A team might not turn a profit because of a client issue, or due to the structure of a fee agreement and the relative scope of work or because they were in the early stages of relationship with a new client and were just learning how to make a profit while meeting new demands and expectations. Most of the teams were unhappy, the staff was divided and the bottom line was a mess.

I realized that we had created seven silos, and a company that was split between the haves and have-nots. Nobody wanted to transfer to another team, even if it was best for the firm. Naturally — they didn't want to lose their bonuses.

Architects are creative people. They are recognized and rewarded in their pre-graduate studies for being creative, and are not, for the most part, motivated primarily by money. By creating a competitive culture based solely on profits, we ignored their internal motivation — creativity. We attempted to motivate them with profitability, something they valued far less. Ultimately, we were not getting the one-of-a-kind, cutting-edge concepts we needed to keep our clients happy and attract new business.

Suddenly, my whole competitive paradigm imploded. Witnessing the breakdown of the competitive process and its impact on our company culture woke me up. Trying to maximize the profits of each team was actually working against maximizing the profits of the entire company! I saw that the only way we would reach our goal and maximize our profit potential was through cooperation, collaboration and working together as *one* team. We made a sweeping change. First, we consolidated the profits and losses of all seven teams. Then we announced that we would pay a bonus to everyone based on the company's net income. Some of the members of the more consistently profitable teams resented me for this decision. But I assured them that, by working together, we would produce extraordinary profits — far beyond what they had known in the past.

By fostering a new model of cooperation and collaboration, we were able to turn the company around. We met our goal of generating enough revenue to allow each of the owners to take home a million dollar annual salary — and we did it in five years, instead of ten. Five years!

Once our staff committed to the new system, there was no stopping them. Working in collaboration, they were able to solve problems creatively and generate brilliant, innovative concepts that helped attract and retain new business. The new system broke down long-held barriers between our architects and our engineers, which enabled *each* group to work more efficiently and increase profits. No longer held back by competitive paradigms, we were able to lead effectively, ultimately taking the company from forty employees in one office to a staff of six hundred in five cities, and generating close to one hundred million in gross billings annually. In an industry that averaged a net income between fifteen and twenty percent, we consistently doubled those profit percentages. Our firm was ranked as one of the most profitable in the industry. By working cooperatively, we surpassed every goal we set.

We all operate within paradigms about how to do business — how to start and run a business, how to grow a business and how to solve problems along the way. Our paradigms are a result of our education, and exposure to traditional models that we thought were successful but were, in reality, simply wrong.

*By fostering a new model of cooperation and collaboration, we were able to turn the company around. We met our goal of generating enough revenue to allow each of the owners to take home a million dollar annual salary — and we did it in five years, instead of ten. Five years!*

After twenty years of just assuming the competitive model was the right approach to motivating people, I learned the hard way that there is a better way to lead. Building competitive teams in the hope of generating increased profits for the company was a symptom of flawed thinking. When I changed my approach, the door to a world of possibility and opportunity suddenly swung open. In other words, we started "managing" processes and procedures and "leading" our people.

This paradigm shift may, on the surface, seem more applicable to one industry over another. In fact, it applies to all. It may be less apparent that a cooperative model will work at a construction company, or a manufacturing company or on Wall Street. Yet in every organization, when each part is working for the good of the whole, there are no barriers to innovation.

What I grew to love most about my job was helping people accomplish goals that they couldn't achieve without my expertise and new perspective. I wanted to assist other underperforming companies in reaching their true potential, building successes and eventually setting and attaining goals they had never previously imagined. In 2003, I left the corporate world to start my own consulting practice. I researched cooperative thinking: how upper, middle and lower management could work together to achieve great success. I participated in CEO conferences that taught business leaders about the cooperative business philosophy, and coached them in implementing it within their own ventures.

Despite my experience, I still firmly believed that competition *between businesses* was healthy, appropriate and even necessary. I thought I had seen it all, and that the concept of cooperative business sounded too good to be true. Nevertheless, my previous success with the cooperative model eventually persuaded me to try it.

I began to give advice freely to anyone and everyone who asked. Those whom I could not help I referred to someone who could, even though it meant I might not benefit financially. I applied my hard-earned cooperative thinking approach to my interactions with other businesses, even though at first it seemed I might be giving away business. Within a year, though, I had several new clients. Soon I was receiving requests from all over the country for my services. I had not thought it possible to experience a pivotal paradigm shift *again*, but I did.

By adopting a cooperative business model, I tripled my net profit in three years. Today, I consult with companies ranging from firms with multi-million dollar budgets to new inventors working out of their garages — and everyone in between. The more I give freely, the more I receive. Just as our architects and engineers worked together for the good of the company, earning huge individual bonuses, I work *for the good of all* — and watch in amazement as new opportunities and increased profits come rolling in.

Competition stifles creativity and limits opportunity. Ultimately, this leads to a poorly performing bottom line and a lack of motivation. Cooperation is the great motivator because it frees people up. When you're not thinking about how to get a leg up on "the competition," you have actual space and imagination available to innovate, create, focus and maintain your enthusiasm for your company and your goals.

It took me nearly thirty years to shift my competitive paradigms. Once I did, I never looked back.

*Harry Lay is a trusted advisor to* CEOs *and business leaders worldwide. He worked in the public accounting sector for nineteen years with three firms, two national and one local. While he was President and* CEO *of an international architectural and engineering firm, that firm oversaw the full creation process — from design to building to opening — of all the stores built in the* US, *from 1990–96 by one of the world's largest retailers. Leveraging his experience in the public and private sectors, Harry has enjoyed facilitating seminars for professional associations and private companies. He has been featured in* Fortune *and* The Wall Street Journal, *serves on numerous Boards of Directors and is a faculty member of* CEO SPACE, *a national association for* CEOs.

# The Trifecta

ADRYENN ASHLEY

Like any "get 'er done" entrepreneur, I was once a pro at going solo. Whatever needed to be done, I did it; and then I did everything else, too. Need a great idea? Just give me one minute. Need a genius marketing plan? No problem, I'm on it. Need someone to execute the plan flawlessly? Consider it done.

It's the nature of the beast, really. Most first-time entrepreneurs face the monumental task of pulling off major miracles from scratch with little or no help. We get used to seeing our own name next to every task on the "volunteer sign-up sheet" that is our massive to-do list. Even when I hired assistants to help me with this or that, I still felt like the captain, first mate and crew of my own ship.

While this approach certainly wasn't practical on any level, the *real* problem was there was no one to tell me when I drifted off course. And boy did I drift!

In my second year of working on a dark, depressing, soul-sucking documentary about fathers' rights and the child-support industry, I realized I was totally unhappy. If you knew me, you would know that I don't do unhappy. I'm always bubbling with positive energy, so to find myself actually using the D-word — *despair* — was quite unusual territory for me. It was as if I was experiencing a mind-meld with the subjects of the documentary, despondent individuals with whom I spent most of my time — first in person, and then for hours on end as I spliced together their tragic stories in my editing room.

One day, I noticed an ad announcing an event for entrepreneurial women. At that point in my life, I never went anywhere alone, so I dragged my friend Claire with me for moral support. It seemed like a good idea for both of us — I needed something besides my documentary to focus on, and Claire was an up-and-coming brander who could use a few contacts.

When we walked into the event, we were stunned to find three hundred women dancing like they had no worries — no bills, no fears, no responsibilities. Leading the group was Allie, a perky blonde who reminded me a lot of how I *used* to be. Vivacious and carefree, she danced like she was not, in fact, wearing business casual and three-inch heels.

*I was stuck captaining a ship I had no business being on, and here was a woman who appeared to be completely at ease leading hundreds of total strangers.*

Allie mingled with the celebrity guests who breezed in to inspire us, and every time she took the stage she made us all feel like all of our dreams were possible. I looked up from my front-row seat and thought, "I need some of that!" I needed some of the inspiration and energy Allie radiated. I needed leadership. I was stuck captaining a ship I had no business being on, and here was a woman who appeared to be completely at ease leading hundreds of total strangers.

During the break, Claire and I made a beeline for Allie. In my serious case of hero worship, I couldn't help myself — I gushed. Allie listened attentively as I bubbled over with ideas she'd inspired, so many that Claire whipped out a micro-recorder to capture the million-dollar business plans streaming from my mouth. Claire, recently laid off, had been toying with the idea of launching her own branding business. Right there and then she committed to doing it, and we wowed her with our enthusiastic support. Allie was equally receptive as I shared the abridged version of my own story, and what I had hoped to achieve with my documentary: to shed light on issues I had experienced in an effort to effect positive change.

Here was a woman who seemed to have it all, who looked like

she had all the answers. So I felt compelled to share my frustrations with her about how the universe seemed to set up roadblocks at every possible turn, and how, ultimately, the experience had given me a serious case of the blues. "Wow. That sounds like a chore, not a labor of love," Allie offered. "What did you love to do before you took on this documentary project?"

Good question, I thought. And then, without missing a beat, I answered it. The truth just poured out of me. I told her I had been fearless once, pulling off major wins on instinct alone. To ensure the success of my films and other projects, I had learned how to market myself. I became a whiz at self-promotion. I was shameless. Spunky. Brave. "So I guess we have a lot in common," Allie said, giving me a big smile. In that moment, I realized I needed more people like Allie in my life — pronto!

Taking a mental inventory of my circle, I tried to come up with names of people who were like Allie in spirit: fun, positive and energetic. I believe that each of us is the average of the five people we spend the most time with. I had been spending my time with bitter, desperate and depressed people, and I was feeling all of that, too. Over the next few months, my fun and energetic friends helped me tell my story in a positive way. They gave me permission to stop working on the documentary. It was as if I had been drowning, and they showed up in a lifeboat saying, "Come aboard. You can let that go now."

Suddenly my path was clear. I hatched a plan to write a book about my experiences, a book that would help women protect their assets and help everyone understand the family court system. I met regularly with Allie and Claire to share fresh drafts of chapters and refine my marketing plan for the book. We reinvented "girls' night out," devoting our time to brainstorming, troubleshooting and encouragement. We were a three-woman cheerleading squad. Each one of us was supportive, always positive, and dedicated to helping in any way we could. It was so much fun, I felt like I had been let out of prison!

On paper, the three of us really appeared to be competitors. After all, we each specialized in some aspect of marketing and self-promotion. Soon the honeymoon would be over, and the catfights would begin, right? Wrong! We just kept helping each other stay on our true paths. We opened doors, and knocked down a few, too. And we've had an absolute blast together. Bye bye, darkness. Hello, happy girl. I remember you.

---

*"Wow. That sounds like a chore, not a labor of love," Allie offered. "What did you love to do before you took on this documentary project?"*

---

As I prepared my book for launch, I realized I loved, loved, loved helping people learn how to do their own self-promotion. In 2006, I launched Wow Is Me!, and began teaching other authors and entrepreneurs the art of shameless self-promotion. I was finally in my zone, but more importantly, I was not alone. Wow Is Me! has grown tremendously because of my girls' support. Over the years we have all relied heavily on each other in our ventures, referring clients to one another, brainstorming ideas and helping each other stay on course. When Claire and Allie have clients who need a crash course in self-promotion, they send them over to me. Or, if one of them has a client who wants someone to promote them, I am the first person they call. On the flip side, if I determine that a new client isn't ready for prime time, I send that person over to Claire for her magic branding touch first. Or, if one of my clients lacks sales savvy, I refer her to Allie to learn how to make a sale.

In most business relationships, there is an implied agreement that every contribution be equal. Our relationship has been successful because we have always had the understanding that we give what we can give — and that will always be enough. There is never a measuring stick attached to our support. Allie is fond of saying, "There is more than one chocolate chip cookie!" In other words, there is room for all of us. We never compete for the same clients — we each use all of our best skills to help those clients achieve their goals. The more clients we "share," the more clients we gain. It is as if our energetic, enthusiastic collaboration attracts people to us.

I call our group "The Trifecta." In betting on horse races, placing a trifecta bet requires you to choose the winner *and* which horses will place and show. Or, the first, second and third place horses, in order. "The Trifecta" describes us perfectly because we are all winners, and because I know that the three of us racing together will always take all three top spots. Since our first collaboration, we have worked together on many projects. Allie and Claire's latest venture, The Hatch Network, was created in response to all of the requests they received from entrepreneurs looking for more specific, concentrated help. They shuttered their individual businesses and launched this new idea, helping entrepreneurs hatch their dreams.

As part of The Trifecta, I am more powerful than I was solo. Now, after years of mastering collaboration and cooperation, I am stronger, faster and smarter. In a group, we fill in each other's blanks, sing each other's praises and rise to each other's challenges. And we dance. We dance like no one is watching.

And what became of my one-woman band? I put it up on eBay and called it a day. Just because I *can* do it all, doesn't mean I should. Neither should you.

*Adryenn Ashley is an award-winning filmmaker, parallel entrepreneur (as in simultaneous multi-brand launches) and unabashed author who achieves the impossible: using laugh-out-loud humor, she delivers essential business and marketing information so effectively, you actually get it! A Certified Asset Protection Specialist and Forensic Accountant, she breaks down complicated business issues into step-by-step achievable processes, empowering entrepreneurs to grow empires. As an actress, she is used to transforming herself and others into riveting onscreen characters. Now she uses her well-honed techniques to transform everyday entrepreneurs into wildly successful business celebrities.*

*Adryenn is the author of the award-winning bestseller,* Every Single Girl's Guide to Her Future Husband's Last Divorce, *and the forthcoming* Spotting the Kooks.

# The Bridge between "Us" and "Them"

KATHIE BOBBITT

What is a business, but the sum of all its parts? A system of individuals — each fully empowered and supported in pursuit of the common goal — creates a strong, sustainable venture. Fear, on the other hand, is not a component of a solid work ethic. And yet it has been woven into the fabric of relations between workers and management in the competitive business world for generations. As a culture, though, the business world is waking from this long sleep.

CEOs and their colleagues and employees are discovering that the Law of Business Attraction is for everyone. From the least-skilled and lowest-paid employees on our teams to business owners and their top-tier managers, everyone involved is benefiting from this exciting approach to the business model. Why? Because in a truly cooperative business venture, potential for growth continues to increase rather than reaching a plateau.

Cooperative business *should* benefit business owners and CEOs — and it does. But it isn't just about CEOs doing what it takes to get ahead; it's about cooperation between *everybody* involved. In fact, it would be impossible for a business to succeed without a system of support for all the players on its team. And this system must be based on compassionate awareness, not on fear.

We are all connected. When we treat others poorly, we treat ourselves poorly. I know this from many years of direct experience. As a young woman in the Air Force, I pushed myself to achieve great things. My own growth and goals in that system were under stress, though, from the constant effort to be recognized and taken seriously as a woman in a "man's world."

Later, I witnessed a similar dynamic during many years of work as an independent consultant for a company that had contracts with a number of manufacturing plants. My job was to go into a given plant, look at the products and manufacturing processes being used to produce them and determine whether or not the plant was generating products safely and up to standard. Each product going out the door required a specific mark of approval, which was my responsibility. For me, the most important part of my job was working cooperatively with the engineers, the plant managers and the people who worked so hard to get their product out the door. Without all of us communicating and making an effort together, we had no way of guaranteeing the safety of our products or of the consumers who bought them. I felt proud to be in a position to safeguard consumers.

*CEOs and their colleagues and employees are discovering that the Law of Business Attraction is for everyone.*

And yet, because of the punitive culture that had evolved in some of the plants, many times I was viewed as an enemy there, rather than a support. Instead of each individual worker being empowered to do her best to make a safe product in a reasonable time and fashion, workers were churning out products as fast as they could, not because they cared, but to avoid punishment. And when I came into a plant and found that a product or a process was unsafe, I (necessarily) disturbed this established pattern.

I witnessed an episode at one plant, for example, in which a worker had not turned on a particular safety-testing machine. Management went into an uproar, not because they were concerned about the product but because I was not supposed to see this happening. They were afraid they would look bad, so they decided to shift the blame onto the "dumb woman on the floor."

Instead of embarrassing management or the worker, I helped them to understand that it was to their advantage to design a system that would assure that she remembered this and all other parts of her testing process. It became a positive learning experience for all of us. This cooperative, collaborative model became the hallmark of the work that I did with our clients.

*The most important part of my job was working cooperatively with the engineers, the plant managers and the people who worked so hard to get their product out the door.*

In another plant, I watched the face of a worker, sitting at a machine all day long, pulling a handle. He looked miserable and resentful. The only goal offered the worker by his higher-ups was that of trying to get as many products out as possible. This was not sufficient incentive for him to feel proud of or invested in his work. To add insult to injury, someone was there, standing over him, counting the number of pulls he made on the machine. He pulled the handle as fast as he could to avoid harassment, but the moment management left him alone his work became sloppy. He could not have cared less what the numbers were. Management took no responsibility for the disrespect and lack of appreciation shown to its workers. This particular worker's disrespect for his job reflected to management the corporate culture that they had established.

Later, in the break room, I approached the handle-puller. He complained about his job, the management that disrespected him, and the company. His body language was taut and angry. And as he talked about the difficulties in the rest of his life, it seemed to me that the negative beliefs — propagated in his relationship to his work — had seeped into every aspect of his life.

The Law of Attraction shows us that we get to choose what we create in our lives. But for the most part, people don't understand that. The plant worker who felt so disempowered could not even imagine it. For the most part, we're not taught that we are responsible for creating our lives in every moment, and for each interaction we have with others. Instead, many people tend to shift responsibility away from themselves by thinking, "If he would just get his act together, I would be okay." It happened at all levels and with almost everyone at the plants — managers and floor-workers alike.

When we blame others for things we create in our lives, when we fail to take responsibility, then we have no perceived power — and therefore no personal power. We are unable to respect each other enough to work cooperatively, or see that each person has her own important place in a functioning system. That's why the Law of Attraction is so important to share: so that people can begin to understand that they have the capability to *choose* in their lives.

My experiences in the plants, and my efforts to help establish cooperation among plant staff for the safety of its customers and the greater good of the company, were what ultimately inspired and qualified me to follow a higher purpose. Today, my work is focused on helping companies restructure, accept responsibility, communicate and lead with compassion. I coach businesses to create truly cooperative systems. These environments empower each individual to become creator of his or her own rich life — and co-creator of dynamic, successful businesses in which everyone benefits and reaps rewards.

---

*For the most part, we're not taught that we are responsible for creating our lives in every moment, and for each interaction we have with others.*

---

My work gives back to me tenfold. I now have a delightful and powerful network of clients, allies and friends. One client, a CPA who has become a close friend, is a case in point. After we completed his strategic plan, I introduced him to people in our area to help him to implement it. Through my contacts in the local Chamber, I connected him with the Chamber's executive director — and to other people with whom he built useful alliances. I also suggested him to some of my other clients. With the help of others, and by virtue of his own willingness to share his ideas, he has succeeded in stepping outside the box he had been thinking and working in. He is realizing his goal. And, in appreciation of our partnership and respect for my work, he referred me to one of his clients who has also completed a strategic plan.

Through building the success of my colleague's organization, I fostered the success of my own community and my own business. In promoting win-win relationships, I have become known for caring about others and understanding what it takes to create abundance in business. The benefits to my company, and my clients' companies, increase exponentially. I see it every day.

*Kathie Bobbitt is President of Kinesis Development LLC, a life and business leadership training company that bases its work on core beliefs, leadership principles, wealth consciousness and strategic and business planning concepts. She is co-creator of www.consciousaccountability.com, a website coming in 2009 for conscious CEOs and entrepreneurs. She is also a business success coach and organizational trainer, a Peak Potentials Certified Trainer, a Certified Entrepreneur with IBI Global's CEO Space and an affiliate of Resource Associates Corporation and Total Quality Institute.*

*Kathie served in the United States Air Force and was chosen by Greenville Talk as one of Greenville, South Carolina's 2007 Twenty-five Most Beautiful Women, based on her efforts to help make her community a better place to live. She is married and has two married children and a grandson.*

# I Don't Believe in the Law Of Attraction

GREG WRITER

Even though I've made this supposed law work for me in my business and in my life, I don't believe in the "Law of Attraction." My reason is simple: I can't find the Law of Attraction anywhere in the Bible. What I do find is the Law of Faith.

The Bible tells us that the spirit of giving offers fulfillment; that you reap what you sow. This is very similar to the philosophy of the Law of Attraction, which I believe comes from God's word. The scripture that comes to mind is Proverbs 23:7, "As a man thinketh in his heart, so is he." Though the Law of Attraction is not mentioned in the Bible directly, the beliefs are at least partly rooted there.

As the Law of Attraction has inspired so many people to give freely to others with no thought of personal gain, the Bible has inspired me to do the same. The spirit of collaborative business is built on these principles. How can I help you? How can I be of service to you? When everyone is of the same mindset, we reap tremendous rewards in the form of guidance, strategic partnerships and even investment capital. Early in my professional life, I succeeded in highly competitive industries, but I knew I did not belong there. Now, I cooperate and collaborate, giving freely of my time and energy. My most important venture — my passion project — is the Children's Educational Network (CEN).

---

*Though the Law of Attraction is not mentioned in the Bible directly, the beliefs are at least partly rooted there.*

---

Seven years ago, my young daughter typed her name into a search engine, which took her to a pornographic site. I was appalled! More, I was furious. Determined to find a way to protect innocent children from pornography, violence and hate on the Internet, I developed the first private-label Internet browser, designed to let children explore the Internet safely, surfing to pre-approved websites.

Because I have learned collaborative business techniques, I was able to develop a cooperative marketing strategy that allowed me to seek high-level partnerships for CEN. For example, we have a version of our software featuring characters from the movie, *Shrek*. In collaborating with a major film studio (co-founded by Steven Spielberg), using iconic imagery from its hit animated feature film, we were able to attract interest from more families, thereby creating safe Internet experiences for more children.

It took a year and a half to get a signed contract for the *Shrek* browser for kids — I spent months trying to get my foot in the door at DreamWorks, but once they saw the win-win possibilities, the process moved quickly. The partnership was a win for DreamWorks, too. The *Shrek* brand benefits from the association with Internet safety. Do you see what collaboration can do?

*"As a man thinketh, so is he." Because I thought I could, I did!*

Competition was part of my life from an early age. Born into a wealthy family, I began my *Rich Dad, Poor Dad* life when my parents divorced. I lived with Mom and visited "rich" Dad on weekends. On one side I lived, tasted and enjoyed wealth; on the other I was surrounded by financial struggles, sacrifice and hard work for little or no pay. As I matured, I was driven to make my life a financial success and follow in Dad's footsteps. After reading the book *Think and Grow Rich*, I actually set the goal to become a millionaire by thirty and a billionaire by the time I hit forty.

"As a man thinketh, so is he." Because I thought I could, I did! Dad suggested investing in stock. My first investment turned two thousand dollars into fourteen thousand in three short months. I had found my calling! I got my stockbroker's license and became a licensed money manager. Though I knew nothing about money and investing, I had dozens, and later hundreds, of accounts for which I recommended investments to investors!

At twenty-one, I bought the firm I worked for and became the youngest owner of a full-service investment banking firm in the history of the United States. It was a dog-eat-dog business. I was taken advantage of many, many times because of my young age and naiveté. No one in that industry was there to help me succeed; in fact, their success required that I fail. I was on my own, working multi-million dollar deals every day. It wasn't long before I realized I could not be as cutthroat as the leaders in this industry. After going through the crash of 1987 — wherein I lost a million dollars in my trading account in one day — followed by the Savings and Loan debacle, I had had enough of the VERY competitive investment banking business.

In my new life as a marketing consultant, I taught a marketing system called "Monopolize Your Marketplace" with the motto, "Crush your competition." I did very well teaching entrepreneurs how to do just that. But as time went on, I realized that this crushing your competition thing was just not me.

When I eventually began incorporating cooperative business methodologies into my business ventures, I was AMAZED how effective cooperation could be when put into action. The more I gave freely to others, the happier I was. I felt revived and had a new sense of energy about business. Instead of feeling stressed, I felt excited, and rather than feeling jaded about business, I felt a sense of unwavering optimism.

Collaborating with people to help them achieve their goals and dreams was a fantastic awakening for me. It resonated with me on a deep level, and as a Christian. We truly do reap what we sow. It reminded me of the words of my mentor, Zig Ziglar: "Help enough people get what they want and you will get what you want." However, in experiencing the joy of helping others with no thought of my own personal gain, the concept reached a whole new level. This was my true nature all long, as it is YOUR true nature. As I continued to enjoy helping others, I felt more important and more fulfilled in my life.

My whole corporation, CEN, was built on the cooperative model. My goal was to make a significant difference in the world, while at the same time create a successful company. The light bulb moment was when I realized that if I engineered the technology for private labeling, I could work with countless companies, celebrities and organizations to get the software in the hands of families who needed it. In collaborating with others to market and sell the software, I created a business model that was dependent on cooperation — combining my multi-million dollar platform with the power of existing brands.

---

*In collaborating with others to market and sell the software, I created a business model that was dependent on cooperation — combining my multi-million dollar platform with the power of existing brands.*

---

When you are focused on collaborating and have faith in the outcome, you attract amazing opportunities. For example, when Lauren Nelson, Miss America 2007, announced her platform of protecting children online, we approached her with an idea to partner with CEN. Together we created the Miss America Kids Safe Browser similar to the McGruff Kids Safe Internet Browser we created with the National Center for Crime Prevention. The next thing I knew, she was on Fox speaking with Bill O'Reilly, and on other network news programs, and was featured in thirteen thousand newspapers, talking about Internet safety and our browser. Thanks to the cooperative model, six thousand children received the software for free and are being protected every day.

Most recently, I signed an agreement with Time Ventures, a subsidiary of TIME, Inc. It will offer our software to protect children on the

Internet as a premium gift for everyone who subscribes to one of its many magazines. It is a win-win for all parties. Also, our partnership with TIME, Inc. adds credibility to CEN, and TIME, Inc. is able to show it cares about families and Internet safety.

There are dozens, hundreds, thousands of stories just like mine, of people who engaged in cooperative business and achieved amazing results. Whether you believe in the Law of Attraction, the Law of Faith or both, remember at the core of these laws is the fundamental truth: you reap what you sow.

Begin by asking, "How can I help you?" Then, watch doors open that you never new existed.

*Greg Writer is the CEO and founder of Children's Educational Network, dedicated to safely opening up the educational power of the Internet to children. With nine years in the Internet safety industry, Greg created one of the first technologies designed to protect children online using the "Include List" methodology, which is reported to be the safest and most reliable method for keeping children safe while they use the Internet. Visit www.childrenseducationalnetwork.com for more information or to download the safe browser. He recently developed Club TUKI, a safe environment for online play where children can have fun while learning the financial skills they will need as adults. For more information, please visit www.clubtuki.com.*

*Greg is an executive with more than twenty years of experience in corporate finance, capital formation, executive level management, mergers, acquisitions, software development and sales and marketing. His company Internet Oil Wells teaches people how to supplement their income online. For more information, visit www.internetoilwells.com.*

# Cash Crash to Conscious Creation

## The Seven Secrets to Your Conscious Creations

SHANNON BURNETT

At the age of twenty-five, when most people are enjoying their friends and exploring endless opportunities, I suddenly became a single mom with two young children. Forced to survive on my own, I eventually took a job in sales. I did it all — endless marketing letters, cold calls, networking meetings. I even went door to door. I was miserable, and felt there must be a better model for doing business.

I soon began to attend business-networking events — but felt like an orange in a barrel full of apples. I was very focused on all of us working together to help each other out, whereas everyone else was in it for himself or herself. Throughout all of this, I was working on my spiritual self, too — that is, I was just as interested in making myself a better person as I was a better businesswoman. Then something amazing happened.

I realized that being a better person and being a better businesswoman go hand in hand. I saw that, the better a person I was, the better a businesswoman I would be — and vice versa. In light of this revelation, I wondered if I could create a company in which every business interaction was a cooperative partnership of heartfelt proportions. I wondered if, with this approach, I could lead my community and thus the entire business world into a better way. And even if I could, I wondered if the business world was ready for this — and if I was worthy of such a responsibility.

I soon got to work. I knew there had to be others who felt as I did, and I believed that if I began to act on my vision, others would be eager to join me. I started by writing down every idea I could think of to bring my vision to reality. Eventually, I created Conscious Living

Partnership (CLP), a vehicle to bring heart and soul into networking, to lead and support personal growth and to teach others the power of collaboration.

Then came the hard part — putting these powerful concepts into action in order to attain a conscious creation. I was a single mother on welfare with no experience in building a business. How was I going to inspire powerful, dynamic, and influential leaders to join me in my mission? First, I surrounded myself with successful role models. I found an expert in every area of my life, including finances, personal growth, family life and health, and did what he or she did in order to achieve similar results.

*I realized that being a better person and being a better businesswoman go hand in hand. I saw that, the better a person I was, the better a businesswoman I would be — and vice versa.*

Success comes much more easily when you commit to finding role models who are living the life you desire. That is my first secret to conscious creation. My second secret is to be willing to ask for help. After all, that's why we have role models — for guidance and help. None of us is truly ever alone, so there's no sense pretending we are. Some people think asking for help is a sign of weakness, but they're wrong. Asking for help requires complete confidence in who you are and what you're doing. Only people who feel inferior or have doubts are reluctant to ask for help.

To do all this, I needed to be willing to stretch beyond my comfort zones; this is my third secret to conscious creation. Growing can be painful or difficult, and sometimes just plain embarrassing, but if we're not growing, we're dying. So every day I had to renew my commitment to being a perpetual student of life, constantly availing myself of new experiences, new knowledge and, ultimately, new wisdom. I continue to renew this commitment every day.

Throughout this whole process, I kept listening to my heart, even when it didn't make sense — my next secret to conscious creation. I had plenty of people telling me I wasn't going to pull this off. On some days I even had *me* telling me I wasn't going to pull this off. But that was the logical me, and for what I wanted to do, logic simply didn't matter. It couldn't. From Henry Ford to Gandhi to Oprah Winfrey, our greatest visionaries have always had to defy logic to achieve their dreams. So did I, and so will you.

---

*Asking for help requires complete confidence in who you are and what you're doing. Only people who feel inferior or have doubts are reluctant to ask for help.*

---

Just keep listening to your heart, and you can't go wrong. Logic has limitations; your heart doesn't. In order to achieve your dreams, you must be the power and voice for change. Not somebody else. You. And if you listen to your heart, you will be. After all, all logical thinking is the same for everyone, so if you're thinking logically, you won't be unique. But if you're thinking with your heart, you will separate yourself from the pack, and then what matters is not the size of your vision, but the level of your commitment. This will be evident in your choices. Therefore, consciously choose to make a difference in this world. You can do this simply by sharing a smile with a stranger or, more significantly, by offering your time, talents and treasures for a great cause.

By applying these seven secrets to my conscious creation — surrounding myself with successful role models, asking for help when I needed it, stretching beyond my comfort zones, listening to my heart, and being the power and voice for change — I was able to make the dream of Conscious Living Partnership into a reality, one that continues to grow every day.

It hasn't always been easy. Many days and experiences were particularly hard, but I wouldn't trade one step of my journey for anything, and that includes the days of being a single mom on welfare. Everything I encountered on my own path helped fashion me into the person I am today, which brings me to my next secret for conscious creations: The BIGGER the challenge, the BIGGER the blessings. Those events that seemed like the worst ever often became our biggest blessings. Pay attention to the BIG challenges; they can be your greatest teachers, leading to your greatest breakthroughs.

Almost all of us have had a truly horrible experience — divorce, loss of a loved one, financial hardship or even ruin. At the time, those experiences seemed like the worst things that could ever happen. But by plodding through those experiences, we learned about ourselves, and our world, in ways that would greatly help us in the future — and we acquired tools we probably wouldn't have been able to find otherwise.

Wouldn't it be nice if we could have those great learning experiences and great breakthroughs without going through those really tough events? Sure, and it does happen that way, but tough events are sometimes necessary because they open us up to new thoughts, new experiences, new ways of seeing the world.

*Those events that seemed like the worst ever often became our biggest blessings. Pay attention to the BIG challenges; they can be your greatest teachers, leading to your greatest breakthroughs.*

And that brings me to my final secret to conscious creation, which is that we must realize that the only difference between You and Me is our THOUGHTS. We are all human beings, choosing our different experiences. We are all in this together, and the notion that we're separate is a perception society has created, one that is far from the truth. That is why, when we do something awful to someone else, we feel so lousy; because we're connected, harming another actually harms oneself.

But the flip side to that is the good news: helping others helps us. That's why I founded CLP — to create a community in which individuals build and develop strong, lasting relationships. We all have hearts, feelings, and dreams. And we're all here to experience love, joy, happiness, and freedom. When we work together, every genuine, heartfelt and good goal is much more easily attained.

Are you truly ready to make a difference in your life? Do you have a big vision? If so, then it is time to let go of what you believe to be the "right" way and open your heart in each moment. When you realize the only difference between You and Me is our thoughts, you open yourself up to a new world of unlimited possibilities.

*Founder and CEO of Conscious Living Partnership (CLP), Shannon Burnett has dedicated her life to creating a global network for uniting businesses, individuals and organizations. Because of Shannon's extensive background in public relations, marketing and event planning, CLP successfully promotes national and international speakers, workshops and events. Highly sought after for television, radio and print interviews, Shannon has trained and coached individuals and businesses in marketing, business development and personal growth. Known for her exclusive "Million Dollar Rolodex," she has an incredible ability to connect others so they can do the same.*

# The Dream Team

ELYISSIA WASSUNG

Imagine you have a team of professionals, rock stars in their own fields, backing you up. What can you accomplish with their input that you can't pull off solo? How will your goals expand and change when supported by trusted experts? What dreams will you dust off, pull out of drawers, and dare to reveal when you have the resources to do anything — even the impossible?

A dream team can help you see the big picture, to reach even higher than you imagined. They will support you when you take those pie-in-the-sky ideas and turn them into pure gold.

Working with people who have "been there and done that" helps get your big plans off of your vision board and into your real life. Can you do it alone? Sure you can. But with a dream team backing you up, you can do it faster, bigger and better, which means you are less likely to get discouraged and give up before you manifest the destiny you know is yours.

Your dream team is only a heartbeat away. It's not the stuff of fantasy; it's very real and very possible. When you open yourself up to the possibility of real success, and give generously to others in search of their own success story, the right people — the *perfect* people — will walk into your life, ready to help. I know this is true because it happened to me.

As a child I happily helped my mom whip up chocolate treats in our kitchen, experimenting with recipes and creating interesting designs and packaging. Making and selling chocolate was Mom's solution to a difficult situation.

After a car accident left her unable to commute to work, she kept our family afloat by making chocolate. I loaded the homemade chocolates into a shopping cart and pushed it around my Queens, New York, neighborhood, looking for customers.

Chocolate was a big part of my childhood — and my first business venture, after selling Snoopy sno-cones! So when I decided to start my own business, I went back to my roots, launching 2 Chicks with Chocolate from my own grown-up kitchen. By 2004 the business had moved from my home to a mall kiosk, and in 2005 my passion project expanded to the Internet and multiple kiosk locations, each one offering unique chocolate creations.

---

*Your dream team is only a heartbeat away. It's not the stuff of fantasy; it's very real and very possible.*

---

Although business was good, I had this nagging feeling that I was missing something. I knew I could do more with our brand and logo, and that 2 Chicks with Chocolate had enormous potential — way beyond our current operation. But I couldn't see the next step. I needed serious help envisioning this next level for 2 Chicks, so I signed up for a business seminar, hoping to find the answer. I didn't find it, but I did find a lot of people just like me. During the seminar I spent a lot of time with Pam and Tom, both seasoned entrepreneurs who had experienced amazing journeys in life. The three of us became quite close that week, and I started to feel excited about my business again.

On our last day we shared our plans for the coming months. Tom told us he planned to attend his twenty-fifth high school reunion in New Jersey, my home state.

"We should get together," I said excitedly. "What part of New Jersey?"

"Monmouth County," Tom answered.

"You're kidding. That's where *I live!*" I exclaimed. I thought it had to be more than just a coincidence that his event was set to take place in my little town. And when we discovered that the reunion was gathering just down the street from my house, I knew we were meant to meet.

"Do you know any hotels?" he asked. "I can't find a room anywhere near the reunion."

"Why don't you stay with us?" I offered. "In fact, why don't you come too, Pam? We'll have so much fun!"

They were blown away! After all, we *had* just met. But I really wanted to help Tom out. And Pam too, because by then I knew that she could use a getaway. I felt a strong connection to both of them, and something told me it was meant to be, as if I had called them to me. We had so many giggles over that weekend! With Tom at a reunion event, I took Pam out to one of my kiosk locations at the local mall. I had been struggling with how to position it, how to make it stand out, where to go with it. Pam dove in immediately, getting to know my business and helping me re-bundle and re-merchandise products.

The next morning when I was making coffee, Pam and Tom approached me about my business. "We want to help you figure this out," Pam offered. "Tell us what you can and can't do with chocolate."

---

*People started coming out of the woodwork, and my entire dream team — everyone on my wish list — was assembled in less than one year.*

---

"I can do anything with chocolate," I answered. I told the story of making chocolate with my mom, and how all of the neighbor kids loved to watch us in action and help out. I talked about how I loved to create custom chocolates for customers, even back then. We started brainstorming, and with each passing hour I achieved more and more clarity. I had been thinking too small, trying to distinguish 2 Chicks from the other confectionery and gift basket businesses out there. Pam and Tom helped me see that my business was bigger than that.

"You have to become the Starbucks of chocolate!" Pam declared.

Half a day and two pots of coffee later, we had a concept so thrilling, so huge, I could hardly contain myself. 2 Chicks with Chocolate would become a national chain of stores where, in addition to purchasing premade boxed chocolates and gift sets, customers could let their sweet teeth run wild while creating their own chocolate-based concoctions on an interactive assembly line.

I had a new goal and it felt right. I just knew in my gut that it was 2 Chicks with Chocolate's ultimate destination. I gave my new friends a great weekend away, and they helped me find my true calling. But the "*Starbucks of chocolate?*" How would I pull *that* off? Feeling overwhelmed, I hired a business coach and signed up for more seminars. If I was going to play in the big leagues, I needed to get educated — fast.

In the first business class I took after that fateful weekend, I was instructed to make a list of people I wanted around me to support me in my project. List anybody in the world, the instructors said. List your dream team, and they will magically show up. I thought my instructors were crazy. I was lucky enough to meet Tom and Pam, but how was I going to meet the superstars in my own industry *and* convince them to get on board with my big dream?

I did it anyway, creating a dream team that included someone from Disney who knew how to handle licensing; someone from Hershey's who knew the chocolate market; a master chocolatier who could assure supreme quality on a massive scale; a marketing whiz who knew the ins and outs of branding and an executive who had experience with mergers and acquisitions.

To my surprise, we had a former Hershey's executive on board within weeks. Weeks! To my further amazement, when we brought him on he said, "You've got the tiger by the tail. You will be the next big brand in confectionery." People started coming out of the woodwork, and my entire dream team — everyone on my wish list — was assembled in less than one year. Before I knew it, we had forty people working on 2 Chicks with Chocolate. The concept we banged out in my kitchen now had magic and motion under it, with each member of the team bringing added energy and momentum to the project. Since that first meeting with Tom and Pam, I have been mentored by powerful people who have given me their time to the tune of seventy-five-thousand dollars in free services — all before I raised a dime of capital.

Today, with our first 2 Chicks with Chocolate retail store poised to open in 2009, I am amazed at how my business has evolved. What was once just Mom, little me and a shopping cart full of chocolates is now a phenomenon in the making. I never knew it would be this big.

By giving of myself freely, without any thought of reciprocity, I manifested Tom and Pam, two people who helped me get ultimate clarity and come out of my business funk. And by putting my faith in the Universe I called forth my dream team, dozens of rock stars in various industries who have taught me how to take my business from a mom-and-daughter shop to an empire.

I'm a firm believer in giving back tenfold. As I manifest the dream born in two kitchens, I make time to coach start-ups. The more I help, the more good things come to me. And I am blessed with surprise moments of gratitude, when people thank me for helping them learn how to change their own lives and see bigger dreams and brighter futures.

So — what could *you* do with your very own dream team?

*Elyissia Wassung is the "Chick-in Charge" of 2 Chicks with Chocolate, a chocolate retailer with custom products available online at www.2chickswithchocolate.com. The first 2 Chicks with Chocolate retail store will open in New Jersey in 2010. Elyissia is a co-author of* Protogenia's Diary: Outrageously Successful Women Share Stories and Insights *(compiled by Anne Newell) and* Beating the Bailout Blues: How to Stay Sane When the Market is Driving You Crazy *(compiled by Rosalind Resnick). She volunteers as a business coach for start-up companies in her native New Jersey.*

# Healing the Personal Creates the Cooperative

DR. BRENT W. DAVIS

That which fosters or prevents cooperative success or failure in business is the very same thing that fosters or prevents success in one's personal life. We know that, according to the Law of Attraction, we should be able to use principles of intentional creation to manifest what we desire.

Many of us have spent years in self-development, reading books, listening to motivational speakers and attending seminars and events focused on creating an ability to manifest and attract what we envision for our personal and our business lives. And yet sometimes the manifestation is slow, or seems to evade us altogether.

Even teachers and motivators like Tony Robbins and T. Harv Eker openly state in their courses that a large majority of those attending will not, after they leave, make use of the tools provided for their personal transformation due to subconscious blocks.

We may, for example, have earnest and deep intentions to flourish in the cooperative business model, but we still struggle in communication with others and, for no conscious reason we can identify, find it difficult to manifest meaningful connections. We may come into contact with people who say they're gung-ho about our project but then mysteriously disappear or break deals.

This doesn't mean we're failures, or that the Law of Business Attraction doesn't work, or that it's time to give up on the cooperative model. Quite the contrary. It's a signal that it is time to begin to truly unblock our potential by removing self-defeating subconscious beliefs. Intentional creation can activate the positive Law of Attraction *only* when we do not have subconscious barriers to that happening. And, unfortunately, we have a lot of subconscious barriers. People may say they don't have such beliefs, but what they mean — and what they perceive — is that they don't *consciously* hold them. We are not aware of our *subconscious* limitations precisely because they are subconscious!

Subconscious barriers are feelings, emotions and thoughts which generally express themselves all of the time. These barriers are like a perpetually playing message. Subconsciously held beliefs reflecting states of lack, for example, will broadcast constantly, like a radio playing, "There is lack, there is scarcity, I cannot receive," twenty-four hours a day. That is the way the subconscious mind works.

Every week in my clinical practice, I administer initial exams that include screening the subconscious minds of my patients by using applied kinesiology muscle testing to find out where they have self-defeating beliefs. Then we work on clearing these beliefs by "overwriting" and removing them with dynamically positive flower frequencies added in drops to drinking water, which they sip throughout the day. You may think it would take a lifetime to undo the damage of beliefs held tightly in the subconscious, especially those formed in early childhood — but clearing can happen very quickly, and with tremendous results.

---

*When we have obstacles within us,*
*they affect everything around us.*

---

Take, for example, the wonderful story of Mike. Mike is a brilliant engineer, consultant and systems analyst who created an ingenious specialized method for assessing engineering firms. When I first met Mike, he was broke and staying in a weekly rental room. He couldn't find work and didn't understand why.

We went after his negative subconscious beliefs, clearing a whole web of trauma-generated frequencies using the uncut flower essence therapy I invented (and which has been hugely successful and beneficial to many people). Mike was invested in the process, and very rigorous in pursuing his own healing. Mike is now, just a short while later, working with Fortune 500 companies. He is making a great living in terms of money *and* inspiration. Everyone who hires him as a consultant is delighted to collaborate with him, and pays him far more than he ever thought he'd earn. Once Mike shed his self-defeating beliefs, his world opened and filled up. His new clarity touched every part of his life.

When we have obstacles within us, they affect everything around us. These obstacles radiate subconscious messages that keep us from attracting, like Mike, the prosperity we seek. They prevent us from encountering the kind of people we want to collaborate with, and manifesting what we work hard to create. We may consciously understand and cultivate the Law of Business Attraction, but subconsciously push it away.

When we are finally free from negative subconscious beliefs, we are able to soar into the atmosphere of manifestation and success. We begin to function at the highest level possible, and keep attracting energy instead of having it dissipate or disappear. This can happen in our business lives, as we cooperate and collaborate with others. And when it begins to happen for a group of individuals, the possibilities for successful, creative collaboration increase exponentially and serendipitously.

Of course, cooperative business success should be looked at in terms of the big picture. But it is also vital to address each microcosm within that big picture. The work of cooperation starts individual by individual. Each member of a team, in order for the team to function, must do the work of healing himself or herself by clearing away negative subconscious beliefs. Ideally, awareness and support within a cooperative group will allow for each member to examine the ways in which his or her particular characteristics either favor or hinder joint ventures and creative alliances. If not, the first member of a group to embark on this journey of self-awareness and healing can help transmit her clarity to the *entire* group.

If a person feels very defensive or feels the damage of emotional or physical abuse or trauma, that carries a frequency that could interfere in interactions with other people. The person may have developed adaptations from childhood that render him unable to be present, feel deep communion with others, or focus in a business environment that requires it. Often, because that person feels unsafe, he develops defensive postures that are obstructive to cooperation and can be deal-breakers.

When a person feels threatened, she may develop a reaction of needing to be in control. She has to control events so that something undesirable will not happen. This is anathema to the idea and ideal of collaboration and cooperation. How can we truly cooperate if someone in our group is reacting from subconscious beliefs and unable to curb his or her controlling behavior?

---

*When the receiving process of an individual is placed back on line, it often marks the beginning of empowerment and manifestation for a whole group.*

---

Again, having experienced trauma and its resulting negative subconscious patterns is nothing to be ashamed of. It's common; it's human. When it expresses itself, it's always counterproductive. But it doesn't have to be. Transformational flower frequencies are an astonishing, new, safe and rapid way to reduce its effects.

Maria, a mid-level manager, was a Nashville patient of mine. I provided her with specific flower frequencies to clear her subconscious beliefs relating to her lack of worth. This was helpful in all areas of her life — most urgently in her professional life, since she was outrageously overworked (sixty-to-seventy hour weeks) and underpaid.

Frequencies I discovered in a flower from South America actually enable receiving, and it worked for Maria! I advised the "new" Maria to send out her resumé to find a more rewarding work environment.

When alternative job offers started to roll in, Maria was sad; she really loved the people where she worked and didn't want to leave. After we had another clearing session where she received her final set of flower frequencies, Maria met with the owners of her company and told them what she needed in order to stay. Perhaps because of her clarity, her newfound freedom from releasing "baggage" of the past, and the non-defensive posture she used while communicating with the owners (people who had clearly been taking advantage of her), they began to actually *see* her for the first time. And the next time I saw Maria, she told me she was still working at the same job — but for twice the pay and in forty-hour weeks! Maria's willingness to heal ultimately opened a way for abundance, sharing and cooperation in her workplace — where none had existed before.

When the receiving process of an individual is placed back on line, it often marks the beginning of empowerment and manifestation for a whole group. Our most influential thought leaders have students who may also benefit greatly from employing these flower frequencies. I create custom transformational blends tailored to the work of different teachers in the personal growth movement. Each teacher's specific approaches to life enhancement are expressed through unique flower frequencies formulated exclusively for him or her. So, together, we further the reach, power and success of all of these motivational leaders — while avoiding competitive conflicts!

I have seen countless times that when we are free from internal sabotaging beliefs, the practice of intentional creation has a real chance of activating the positive Law of Attraction. I feel blessed to have witnessed its positive effects in my own life, and in the lives of so many others.

*Dr. Brent W. Davis has been in practice as an integrative healer and holistic chiropractor for over twenty years. He studied at* UCLA, *graduated cum laude from Southern California University of Health Sciences and did his post-graduate studies in classical homeopathy at Hahnemann College of Homeopathic Medicine, under the tutelage of the renowned Indian homeopath K.O. George,* HMD.

*Dr. Davis is internationally distinguished for his landmark herbal research. Beginning in 2001, he received two* US *patents and international patents for a new form of flower essence (www.floralive.com), in which the living flower is extracted uncut, thus preserving the full power of living flowers to help heal emotional trauma and remove negative subconscious patterning. He divides his time between his clinical practice in Nashville (www.davisvitalhealthcenter.com) and conducting workshops for health practitioners in the effective use of his new flower frequencies. He also travels the world, consulting with traditional healers and collecting and documenting medicinal plants.*

# Creating Independence Versus Co-Dependence

VINCENT MOLINA

How many times in life have you asked yourself, "If I only knew then what I know now?" Usually when we ask this, it's out of frustration. We ask this at moments when we realize that because we didn't know then what we know now, we've lost time or money or opportunities to serve more people.

Life is full of paradoxes, and one of the most peculiar yet most wonderful paradoxes of all is that the more we serve others, the more we make for ourselves. This paradox is so true that we have dozens of different ways of reaffirming it: "The more you give, the more you receive," or, "What goes around comes around." Some people just say, "As you sow, so shall you reap." But to maximize our potential to serve, and therefore make, we must, with each situation, be able to readily identify what we need to do, when we need to do it, and what resources are required. And herein lies the challenge many businesses face: they do not know enough to know what they need, when they need it, and what resources are required. So they rely on someone else, usually from outside the company, to do *it* for them, whatever *it* is. That costs money. And relying on someone from the outside usually involves a lot of standing around: that is, wasted time.

But there's a bigger problem. Given the opportunity to acquire new skill sets in the workplace, most employees balk. Even worse, given the opportunity to teach new skill sets to colleagues, most employees refuse, out of fear. They think that the minute someone else learns their job, they won't be needed.

Such competitiveness creates unnecessary dependence throughout the company, and that translates into a lot of wasted dollars and misspent hours. Where in life or business have you helped create independence, in yourself or in others?

I've loved pancakes ever since I was a kid. I always used to bug my mom to make them for me until one day it finally dawned on her to teach me how to make them myself. Her instruction freed us both: she no longer had to listen to me nag for pancakes or take the time to make them, and I no longer had to wait for the efforts of someone else in order to have them. My pancake independence benefitted us both.

Independence can start at home with our children. For me, it certainly started at home with my parents. I frequently discuss how my mother and father didn't tell me how to do things, they *showed* me how to do things. They showed me how to make pancakes and spaghetti and dozens of other dishes. They showed me how to tie my shoes, do the laundry, polish the furniture, balance my checkbook and manage my time. They showed me how to be independent. In showing me how to do things, my parents taught me the most effective way to teach others: by showing.

---

*Where in life or business have you helped create independence, in yourself or in others?*

---

My parents were entrepreneurs. In the sixties, my father bought a small fast-food business in Hawaii that he converted into one of the most successful restaurants on the island. People came from all over, even the mainland, to eat at my family's restaurant. My parents' success was hardly a fluke. Every day, my parents worked to make sure each employee was knowledgeable in each aspect of the business. During a shift, my father would teach you your job, but during a different shift, or maybe during down time, he would teach you someone else's job. So if you were in charge of inventory, maybe he would teach you food prep or customer service.

"I'm not trying to replace anyone," he'd tell his employees. "It is to your advantage to learn what other people do here. The business will grow, new people will be hired and you'll be ready to move up because you already know that job." In addition, the business was not dependent upon one person, so if someone couldn't come in one day, the flow of work continued smoothly. The end result was that everyone worked as a team and everyone respected each other's responsibility, thereby creating an efficient machine that could serve more people, achieve higher profits and increase customer satisfaction. The business thrived for twenty years, and all by word of mouth. My parents never spent a single cent on advertising. Because my parents were willing to train others as much as possible, their business was hugely successful. As a result, my mother was able to transition out of the business and pursue other interests. Since she loves to learn, she decided to go to college. My father, meanwhile, stayed with the business, because it allowed him to do what he loved most — be with customers. The more you share, the more you get to do what you love.

---

*Cooperation doesn't enter a company by itself. It comes in the door every time someone shares knowledge with another. And when it does come in, it brings increased results along with it.*

---

It wasn't until I was older that I realized I'd instinctively brought the lessons my parents had taught me into my own world. My first corporate position was entry level. I was eighteen, and a hard worker. As a result, I was often being promoted and earning interim raises on a consistent basis. But I was also a good employee, so I thought nothing of showing my colleagues what I knew. Because of my parents, such teaching came naturally. It did not go unnoticed.

At the time, I was very fortunate to have the Division Manager as my mentor. One day, he called me into his office. He said that, having reviewed my file and watched me interact with others, he noticed I could do something naturally that most people could not. "You can teach a wide variety of personalities to do what you do, and you can do so without the slightest hesitation or fear."

I shrugged. "I'm just doing what I get paid to do," I said.

"That's true," he said, "but in this day and age (the 1980s), most people think that the way to climb the corporate ladder is always and only at someone else's expense. Therefore, most of your peers are afraid of teaching what they know because they think it creates competition for themselves.

What it really creates, though, is a stronger corporate team, which improves the company's bottom line." Cooperation doesn't enter a company by itself. It comes in the door every time someone shares knowledge with another. And when it does come in, it brings increased results along with it.

"I hear you have a birthday coming up," my Division Manager continued. I acknowledged that I did. My twenty-first birthday was two weeks away. I'd been at the company just inside of thirty-six months. "I have a gift for you. In recognition of your ability and willingness to make others stronger and more valuable assets to the company, I'd like to offer you the position of Corporate Trainer."

Of course I took the gift. I was one of the youngest Corporate Trainers in that Fortune 500 Company, and I was in charge of nine employees. I'd never formally been taught how to be a supervisor, but years ago my parents had shown me. And while many of my peers remained reticent about sharing their skills for fear of competition, I continued to rise to the top precisely because of my belief—which I put into practice—that making others stronger makes us all stronger. Never be scared to show what you know. Never be scared to share your expertise. Rather, what you should fear is a reluctance or unwillingness to share your expertise.

This experience eliminated any lingering doubts I might have had about how making others stronger might negatively affect the achievement of my own goals and dreams. And this experience was the first concrete example, in my corporate life, that creating independence in others was key not only to the success of those around me, but also to my success and the success of my company.

I carried this attitude with me through the years and held to it when I founded a management consultant company. Many people think that my attitude hurts my ability to retain clients long-term and increase revenue. I have learned that by helping others to become independent, I have fostered an abundance of referrals and repeat business.

By applying what I teach, my clients have made their businesses more efficient and more lucrative. They build stronger teams; they raise capital; they complete projects ahead of schedule; they increase revenue; they reduce mistakes; they increase results; they take products to market with a higher distribution and gain a higher profitability. So why wouldn't they come back to me for repeat business? And why wouldn't I be willing to share more that I've learned with them?

Just as important as a continued willingness to teach is a continued willingness to learn. In fact, nothing will strangle a company more quickly than close-mindedness or a lack of curiosity. Working at the management and board level, I have had the privilege of providing companies with the knowledge and skills they need to run their businesses independently versus co-dependently. What's more, passing on skills and knowledge has not only saved time and created more success for others, it has come full-circle and done the same for our company. As a result, several years ago, we permanently adopted the tag line: *Creating Independence versus Co-dependence.*

Many times in our lives, we would have known then what we know now if someone would have taught us — or if we'd only been more willing to learn.

I ask everyone to adopt a cooperative model, to share all their knowledge and skills. And I ask them to do it both at home and at the office. After all, our colleagues or employees are hardly more important than our families. Create Independence versus Co-dependence. By doing so, your family and business endeavors will flourish and you will leave a legacy for others to follow.

*Vincent Molina has thirty years of corporate experience. As President of Vincent Molina & Associates, he provides support on the executive and board levels in such areas as business development, corporate affairs and capital acquisition. He also participates in the* USA *Today Small Business Panel online, which serves over twenty million entrepreneurs. His goal is to Create Independence versus Co-Dependence for his clients.*

*As a business strategist, Vincent works closely with his clients to support them in obtaining necessary professional and financial support, and other resources required to achieve success. As a result, his clients and other professionals have dubbed him The General Contractor of Business. Vincent is also the author of* Communicating with a Former Spouse *and founder of the* Communicating with... *book series, designed to break down the common barriers keeping people from achieving personal and business results.*

# The Unseen Business Trap

ED BOGLE

How do you measure the success of your business? Most entrepreneurs would have the same answer: profits. Why not? It seems logical; profits are easy to determine and track. But do they tell the whole story, the *true* story?

If entrepreneurs, CEOs and managers focus primarily on profits, the "logical" gauge of a company's financial health, why do so many businesses fail to achieve their greatest potential? Even the most successful business can go only so far when focused solely on profits.

Fresh out of college, buoyed by a great business education and utterly sure that I could make a great difference, I joined a large company and went through an intense year-long management development program. By the time I was twenty-five, I was in charge of a six-person team tasked with developing strategy for a major financial institution. We built great strategies, although not everyone in the chain of execution was involved in the development, but who had time for all that "hand holding?" The success of the strategies was unprecedented in the industry and I began to speak around the country and write articles for prestigious journals.

By the age of thirty, I was cocksure I knew how to build a business and outsmart the competitors: work hard; focus on profits; clearly target my market and be uniquely different than my competitors; build silos of human resource development, finance, and accounting operations and if I had to, sell my ideas to those needed for execution.

After ten years of internal corporate success, I opened up a consulting practice that led me to join a "big eight" accounting and consulting firm. My task was to build the regional strategic planning and management consulting practice. I knew I had found a place where I could take my ten years of recognized success and apply it to bigger and better projects. I worked across many industries and sizes and types of companies with mixed results. Some worked well, others seemed to lag — but why? The difference seemed to be with the "people problems," not the strategy.

I was privileged to join a team of people led by a world-renowned strategist, Michael Davidson, to begin the process of building and implementing a world-class business strategy process for our clients. Mr. Davidson had done amazing things for his clients, and seemed to do so consistently, but he brought in concepts that seemed somewhat foreign to my definition of good business strategy. Some of those principles he and others introduced I looked at with a jaundiced eye:

"Running a business is not about the money, it's about the people."

"The doers must be the planners."

"Profits can make you stupid and blind to opportunity and threat."

"Business is about making the soft side hard."

Whoa! This was not what I was taught and what I knew would work, but this Brit was smart and highly successful, so I embraced his premise and diligently looked at his process to bring the marginally successful to new heights.

*Even the most successful business can go only so far when focused solely on profits.*

So, armed with this new toolkit and a focus on the entrepreneurial world, I set out to stake my claim to greater results. One of my early clients was a company in the industrial services industry that cleaned and did maintenance for processing plants. This industry was fragmented and fraught with sloppy work that resulted in many serious injuries and even an occasional death. This client had acquired three companies in this industry and we went to work on developing a clear, winning strategy. We involved many of the company's line and field people and spent hours talking to customers about their needs. Ultimately, we landed clearly on a strategy that came from one of the field managers. "The customers are disgusted by the lack of safety and quality in the execution of their work," he explained.

The strategy was born: "We will be the very best at consistent quality and safety in the industry." The initial programs were developed and reviewed by the employees responsible for their implementation and even the customers. The enthusiasm for the "new positions" began to buzz around the company and the stage was set for implementation. A giant wall-size poster of the strategy was hung in the new training center and all employees signed the banner indicating their commitment to the implementation.

The training was intense and expensive, but the processes, once implemented, brought unheard of results in the industry and created great growth and profits for the company. I was in utter amazement at the speed and quality of the company's growth. Profits soared, celebrations abounded, the company became one of *Inc.*'s Fastest 100 Growing Companies, the CEO was the regional winner of *Inc.*'s Entrepreneur of the Year and the company won the Houston Business Roundtable Award two years running. The company became a Harvard Business School case study. The company went public and tripled the share price in a little over three years. Now I knew I had seen the secrets to high growth — high performance companies. It was truly about the people and their ownership of the vision, mission and strategy to get there.

In 1985 Michael Davidson said in an unpublished work:

> *Ten years ago managers did not talk about 'soft' issues – vision, beliefs, purposes, values and people. They discussed 'hard' issues – that is, profits, costs, headcounts, market share, and growth projections. Customers and employees were loyal. However, in a world of accelerating change and unprecedented global competition, issues that once were considered 'hard' are now 'soft,' that is, erratic, unreliable, and subject to unpredictable change. So to create*

*a foundation for planning and for adjusting to change we must make the so called 'soft' issues 'hard,' that is, predictable, consistent, and stable.*

It truly was about "the doers being the planners." Often the best ideas of how to grow your company and improve its value proposition and therefore margins come from the customers themselves and the people closest to them.

Another client I worked with had just taken over as the CEO of a highly-stressed, twenty-two-hundred-employee company that had enormous turnover. The company definitely was underperforming financially and operationally. He knew that turnover had to be reduced in order to fix the company. We updated the company's strategy, but success in its implementation required new levels of employee training and commitment. In developing a strategy to reduce turnover, we learned from line managers and staff that there were many factors for turnover, and passing the blame to others was readily used as an excuse for mistakes. Out of the company's value statements emerged an often-heard statement that "people are our most important asset."

*The collaborative, cooperative approach drove the company from good to great. Strategies exceeded expectations because they were driven by the very people tasked with their implementation.*

"I'll cure part of the turnover," the president of the company said. "We won't fire anyone without my signature." The president espoused the belief that if we had to fire someone our system failed. So before anyone was dismissed from this company, the immediate supervisor would be required to pen a memo to the CEO as to where "we failed" and what corrective action would be taken so we did not repeat our problem. He was certain that the turnover problem was due to one or all of the processes related to hiring: screening, training and development, or mentoring and supervision.

It worked. Turnover dropped to nearly zero; there was an explosion in employee retention, which led to an explosion in customer growth. All of that "soft side" focus garnered astounding results for the company, its customers and employees. Again, the collaborative, cooperative approach drove the company from good to great. Strategies exceeded expectations because they were driven by the very people tasked with their implementation.

Some twenty-five years and seventy clients later, I have evolved my perspective of what makes a company work. I used to focus on return on capital, profits and market share. While critical, those things are merely the result of value for the customers delivered by inspired people who help focus the future of the company. In fact, when asked today how you know when you have a successful strategic plan, I answer, "When your employees can tell you the vision (where the company is headed), the mission (how we serve our customers) and their role in fulfilling those." You then will have a company that integrates human performance with strategy, and if the employees and customers play a role in migrating that strategy over time, you will drastically increase your chances of strategic and financial success and hence profit and growth.

From my perspective, it is clear that people truly want to work for a share of the vision and be a part of a vibrant company where they can participate in shaping the company. This attracts great employees and the best customers. Do not fall into the unseen trap of focus on profits alone, built from the top — your people truly are your greatest strategic asset, the true measure of your company's success.

*Ed Bogle is a strategic consultant and founder of Bogle & Associates. Ed has more than thirty years of strategic and marketing consulting experience with several years as senior practice leader in Arthur Young's (Ernst & Young) South-*

*west Strategic Management Consulting Practice working extensively with the Entrepreneurial Services Group to connect human performance and business strategy.*

*He has worked with and served as a coach to two of* Inc.'s *Entrepreneur of the Year regional winners and has worked with three companies in* Inc.'s *100 Fastest Growing Companies in the* US. *His work encompasses firms ranging from start-ups and emerging entities to the Global 50 enterprises. This work includes breakthrough thinking for high growth strategies, turnarounds, acquisitions and mergers and capital formation. He has spent recent years working extensively in the "clean, green and sustainable" space and coaching companies on "social entrepreneurship."*

*He holds a* BS *in Marketing from Oklahoma State University, completed graduate studies in strategic management at Colorado University and received advanced certification in, and was a principal in the development of, Arthur Young's strategic planning and management methodologies.*

# Prepare
# To Attract

BURKE FRANKLIN

If you want to attract and capitalize on once-in-a-lifetime opportunities, you've got to be ready for them. I'm not just referring to being in the right space emotionally; I'm talking about being completely prepared so that when God/ the Universe/ Allah comes knocking, you are capable of acting *immediately*. And being the right person to make the most of what you receive. This is the difference between wishing and getting results, between wannabes and masters.

Think about it. Are you really ready? *Really*?

What if an investor showed up at your door looking to fund your promising start-up? Would you be able to answer every question he or she asked? Could you pull out a thorough, professional business plan? Have you completed every possible task as well as you can, so that an infusion of capital would go as far as possible? That would be attractive, right?

What if one of Oprah Winfrey's producers called to find out if your story (or product, or program, or charity) would be a good fit for her show? Would you be able to speak articulately about who you are and why Oprah and her audience should care? Are you ready to deal with the deluge of customers or inquiries that would most certainly come your way? That would be attractive, right?

People — investors, customers, partners, reporters, employees — are attracted to those who are most prepared. People are attracted to confidence, to mastery. Be a master of your business, even if it's just an idea, and you will attract the right people and opportunities with very little effort.

A little over twenty years ago a friend asked me to help him create a business plan. Even though I had been in the business world for about thirteen years, I was more a shoot-from-the-hip kind of guy than a plan-it-out guy. Still, my friend had a potential deal with Apple Computer, and I didn't want to see him lose out just because planning wasn't my thing.

The pitch to Apple had to cover all the bases — product, management, finances — the works. Drawing upon my experience writing copy for the Sharper Image Catalog, as well as my experience selling at every level from clerk to office manager to CFO to CEO, I made sure that every component of the plan sold the Apple hierarchy on my friend's business. It worked beautifully and my friend got the deal. I now look at a business plan as a comprehensive 'brochure' designed to sell a business concept at all levels and to many audiences. Thoroughness and success are attractive too.

---

*When the universe provides you with the opportunity, you still have to seal the deal. People are attracted to potential, and the best way to help them see your potential is to be the master of your idea, the master of your business, the master of your dream.*

---

After that it seemed I was a magnet for people who wanted a business plan. I helped a lot of people write some very good plans, and I started to see that those who had a plan now had a clear sense of what to do next to build their businesses — *and* they started to attract investors! And customers. And people who wanted in. It wasn't just because they presented a well-thought-out, detailed document, it was *who they became* as they worked through every area of their business idea inside and out, and backwards and forwards.

The process of creating their plan enabled them to see what they had to offer, where they were going and what investors would be buying. My friend landed the contract with Apple because *he* was ready for it. And he knew he was ready because in preparing for the opportunity he proved to himself and everyone else that he was the right choice. Attractive.

When the universe provides you with the opportunity, you still have to seal the deal. People are attracted to potential, and the best way to help them see your potential is to be the master of your idea, the master of your business, the master of your dream. In 1988 I decided to take my knowledge and expertise and create business plan building software. I used the first version of my BizPlanBuilder® software to get a $210,000 SBA loan to buy an office condo, and then used it again to establish a $750,000 line of credit to develop new software. And it was easy; it was easy because I was absolutely ready to receive that money. I knew exactly what I was going to do with it and my plan made sense to everyone. Being pragmatic and using the right tools are attractive.

*Mastery is about taking the entire art up a notch. Raising the stakes. Expanding your vision. Pushing the envelope.*

I named my company JIAN (jee'-on), a Zen word meaning "master of every art," because I believe that we can master every aspect of our business — *if* we have the right technologies, tools, and people, and if we co-operate.

Many people believe that the evolution of your spirit is the ultimate goal of life, the meaning of the opportunity to live this lifetime. I consider business to be an art. My business is my *dojo*, a place where I develop myself. Your business can be your *dojo*, too — where you can learn your lessons of life. Mature, evolved people are very attractive.

When we achieve mastery of our business we achieve unflappable confidence in our selves and our vision for our business. With that confidence we vibrate at a higher level — in tune with others who can help and support us. Like a guitar chord, all of the strings must be in tune in order to sound good. Also, just as some music compels you to get up and dance, some music does not. Mastery is attractive.

Cooperating with colleagues allows you to benefit from each individual's own mastery. A team gives you the time and space to do what you do best. When you collaborate with other people and businesses the combination of your energies takes your endeavors to a new level, attracting more business for everyone involved. Who are you aligned with? Harmony is attractive.

Mastery is about taking the entire art up a notch. Raising the stakes. Expanding your vision. Pushing the envelope. The entrepreneur's Achilles' heel is often the "do-it-yourself" mentality. Most people think of entrepreneurship as a solo game, but how can you ever be truly ready to take advantage of the gifts you're asking the universe to provide if you're doing it all alone? (And probably trying to reinvent the wheel while you're at it!) Include others. It's attractive.

The Law of Attraction works like a charm when you first define what you want, and then prepare yourself to be the person who would attract whatever it is you want: money, new clients, key partners, great press, recognition. Just as people are attracted to those who are the most prepared, the Universe is more likely to respond to the requests of those who are ready to use its gifts and graces.

*Get real.* Prepare for what can go wrong (Murphy's Law). Who loses if you win? What forces of Nature are working against you? Munchkins? Flying monkeys? Witches? How will you work around them? We've all had things go wrong — no use keeping your head in the sand (or in the clouds). Deal with the negatives — at least acknowledge them in order to demonstrate your ability to navigate as you move forward. Being grounded is attractive.

Getting frustrated when things don't go your way only leads to suffering. You wouldn't walk into a gym and complain about the weights on the machines, would you? What is attractive is an open person, accepting life as it comes — going forward, no matter what! Being happy is attractive.

Prepare yourself for what is to come. You know what you need to do.

The avoid-dance you've been doing isn't getting you any closer to what you want. See a therapist to rid yourself of recurring negative patterns from your childhood. Become a master of yourself, then your art, and then collaborate with others so that together you can be masters of *every* art. Do whatever it takes to prepare for the opportunities that are flowing like traffic on an eight-lane highway.

When opportunity comes, you can make the most of it; you can seal the deal. When you're ready, the opportunity will come, the money will appear and the people will line up to do business with you. So, *are* you ready? Are you *really* ready? If not, what can you be doing now? Have faith and, as Henry Ford said, "Hustle while you wait." Preparation is attractive.

*Burke Franklin is the founder and* CEO *of* JIAN *(jee'-on), and the inventor of Biz-PlanBuilder® (the most popular software package for producing a comprehensive business plan) and many other* JIAN *products. In the past twenty years,* JIAN *has sold two million copies of* BizPlanBuilder®, *and has helped raise several billion dollars through angel investors, venture capitalists, the* SBA *and bank financing.*

*Burke's extensive background in sales, marketing and management spans more than thirty years, and includes an elected position in the White House Conference on Small Business and a nomination for Ernst & Young's "Entrepreneur of the Year" award. A second-degree black belt in TaeKwonDo, Burke is the author of* Business Black Belt, *a book that teaches entrepreneurs how to build and run successful businesses drawing on parallels with the disciplines of a karate master. Burke is a sought-after speaker and regularly appears on television and radio programs for entrepreneurs. To learn more about Burke and* JIAN, *please visit www.jian.com.*

# Social Entrepreneurship at the Speed of Light!

STÉPHANIE GIROUX

My grandfather and uncles were entrepreneurs — masons. Every two weeks a big truck dropped a huge pile of sand in our back yard, and I was ecstatic. I ran into that big dune and played with my Tonka trucks endlessly. And I was enthralled by the way my grandfather and uncles used that sand to literally build their business. Even then, I was intrigued by the multi-faceted nature of entrepreneurship. I was as fascinated watching my uncles build walls, and hearing their stories of travel across North America, as I was watching my mother work in her beauty salon and balance the books. I was also spellbound by the various forms of our earth — sand, clay, soil, trees, mountains, water.

*In order for our dreams to be fulfilled, we have to be ready — mentally, spiritually, emotionally, intellectually and professionally.*

Back to that pile of sand. I vividly remember myself at the age of four, standing in my imaginary desert, facing toward the sun with my eyes firmly closed. Strangely enough, I was imagining myself as a missionary in Africa. I will never be able to explain that vision, but even at that age I felt a need to help the world somehow, a need that has never stopped nagging me.

A love of business, a love of the earth, a desire to help — these three attributes comprise a large part of who I am. It would be many, many years before these essential parts of me combined in a venture that fulfilled my personal and professional dreams, but I never despaired. I knew it would happen one day. In order for our dreams to be fulfilled, we have to be ready — mentally, spiritually, emotionally, intellectually and professionally. If the opportunity to achieve our dream comes before we're fully prepared to capitalize on it, we will only spoil that chance, which may not come again.

At twenty-two, I started on a spiritual and consciousness path which intensified when, at twenty-four, I became a single mother. In between changing diapers and entertaining toddlers (or trying to), I was studying for my business degree. All through those tough times, as a mother, student and eventually a professional, I never stopped seeking my particular purpose in this world.

My professional life progressed. I became a business consultant for technology projects in large enterprises, and for a long time, it was enough. But my kids grew older, and I grew restless. It was time to expand. For years I had networked with entrepreneurs, so I decided I wanted to be an entrepreneur coach, helping my clients to achieve best practices and access the tools they needed. I loved it. At first. It was certainly more dynamic and creative than my corporate job, but somehow I still felt limited, confined. I felt I wasn't contributing enough. Then I was invited to a wedding in India. As much as you humanly can, seize every new opportunity, partake of every new activity, and never judge anything beforehand. You won't love everything you do, and you'll certainly make some mistakes, but it is so much easier to deal with remorse over something you did than regret over something you didn't try.

I'm hardly the first person to note that India is an incredible melange of smells, sights, sounds and sensations. I saw it all there — extreme poverty, breathtaking natural scenery, incredible entrepreneurial energy. I also spoke with a number of people, including businesspeople, teachers and spiritual guides, who explained to me how that uniquely sad and wonderful country worked.

I reached Pondicherry, a beautiful place by the sea where my father had found inspiration for his Master's in Theology work. I wanted to retrace his steps as part of my own spiritual journey. One night, I didn't sleep at all. Shiva, God of Destruction, was tearing down my old life in preparation for something new. Walking on the beach at dawn the next day, I realized my entire understanding of the world had just changed. I now had a holistic view of the world, one that encompassed all my images of India — everything from the beautiful flowers to dogs and cows sleeping in the trash, from the sunrise over the ocean to the impoverished boys playing in puddles of dust. Our job is not to block out what's wrong in this world. Our job is to embrace it. For not until we fully see and understand all the problems can we begin to envision and formulate useful solutions.

*The question is: how do we create a "wealth machine" that fosters the creation and growth of profitable, sustainable local* and *global initiatives?*

I saw that the possibilities inherent in capitalism and evolving technologies could, and should, be harnessed for solutions that support sustainable economical development while meeting the world's humanitarian and environmental needs. Finally, my love of business, my love of the earth and my desire to help became One. When I returned home, my newfound perspective immediately brought a new set of opportunities and unexpected encounters. I established new networks and attended multiple events where I met amazing people. I also contacted ex-colleagues from all over the world and shared my vision. Many of those people not only believe in my project; they're also interested in joining the team.

The Law of Business Attraction acquires incredible velocity when we offer a vision of sustainable global development that supports the creation and sharing of wealth. People who have a solid set of values regarding humanity but who, for years, have felt constrained by their corporate lives because of financial obligations now have an opportunity to make money *and* better the world. And they're taking it.

I'm not naïve. I clearly see the challenges ahead. For starters, there is the balancing act between institutions and people. The objectives of corporations and governments are often quite different from those of environmentalists and humanitarians. And building a strong, local economy with pride in old traditions may not always jibe with globalization and its sweep of new knowledge and various innovations. But I think the answers to these problems lie in the details of our common denominators. After all, everyone wants a fulfilling career, and no one nurtures the personal ambition to be poor. Everyone wants clean air, soil and water — now and for future generations. And nobody wants other human beings to suffer. The question is: how do we create a "wealth machine" that fosters the creation and growth of profitable, sustainable local *and* global initiatives?

I have personally created a business model that will help entrepreneurs and others pursuing sustainable projects. The hope is that, in turn, these people will create enough revenue not only to gain a profit for themselves but also to fund the profitable, sustainable initiatives of other people. My model is heavily dependent upon the Internet, by far the biggest revolution of our era. All over the world, at any time of the day or night, this entity connects people at the speed of light. That's just the beginning of what it can do. And more than a fifth of the world's population is using this tool.

The point is that, given the incredible innovations in our technologies, now more than ever we have the individual flexibility and means to achieve our personal dreams and help others while exacting less of a toll on our environment. And we can do this no matter our social status, buying power or country of origin. The Green movement, social networks and the Internet are just some of the new trends that make it all easier and more attainable than ever before. But you have to constantly be open to all possibilities within you, and the best way to be open is to develop your spiritual life just as rigorously as you pursue your professional goals.

So — are you going to resist improvement or assist it? Henry David Thoreau once said that the mass of men lead lives of quiet desperation. That's kind of a strong statement, but I do think that, sadly, a lot of people remain hidden behind the walls of their day jobs, living unfulfilling lives because they're fearful of disturbing their basic bottom line — providing for their families and their lifestyles.

Instead of being an accomplice in the world as it is, I choose to invent the future. My vision and intentions are clear, and I choose to live up to them by taking actions that will manifest them. What about you?

*Fluent in French, Spanish, and English, Stéphanie Giroux has more than twenty years of work experience, fifteen of them as a business management consultant implementing business solutions and best practices in various industries in Canada, the Netherlands, North Africa, USA and the UK. She is always seeking opportunities to innovate and take a definitive turn for social entrepreneurship.*

# Speaking from the Heart

Emerald Echo

TAMARA BOWMAN

Growing up with asthma, I struggled to breathe. It scared me to say the childhood prayer, "If I die before I wake, I pray the Lord my soul to take." An unforeseen asthma attack could mean going back to where I came from. This awareness begged questions from within my curious and developing mind: Where did I come from? Why am I even here? Why is it so hard for me to breathe? I felt very much alone.

Being petite and skinny, I wasn't first choice when it came to picking teams for athletic competitions. My inhaler was my best friend, my connection to this world. I remember wishing that choosing "teams" meant utilizing different gifts so that *everyone* could win. It wasn't long before I didn't care if I was connected to this world or not. I didn't feel like I belonged. I went through the motions of existing as my soul fell asleep. If I died before I woke, so be it.

It wasn't until after my first marriage and divorce at the age of nineteen that I went away to college and discovered another world. I left behind everything that was familiar. My heart and mind opened as I studied broadcast journalism, and dove headfirst into the study of psychology.

My big questions persisted: What could possibly be revealed that would make life worth living? What makes relationships harmonious? Where was this life of abundance promised in the Bible? I questioned everything, including God. As I felt my soul awakening from its deep slumber, I could breathe easier.

Through a process of deep internal inquiry and release of stored-up grief, my asthma nearly vanished. I then began to notice how magnetically drawn I was to dolphins. I read every article I could find about them. I learned that, in addition to dolphins being considered one of the most intelligent species, they make love for pleasure, just like us. Dolphins love to eat, play and make love within pods, which are cooperative communities. Wow! If ever a creature on Earth embodied Heaven, it would have to be the dolphin. What fascinated me most was the evidence that dolphins possess miraculous rescuing traits and emotional healing power with humans. There was no end to the stories of dolphins' loving impact upon this planet.

*The Law of Attraction brought me to Princess.*

After graduating college with a degree in Broadcasting Journalism and Communications, I went to work for the Orange County News Channel as an account executive selling air-time commercials. Within a year, my sales reached a peak and I won a round-trip ticket to anywhere in the world I wanted to go. I was so excited and grateful that I could hardly contain my exuberance! I leapt for joy, thinking, "I'm going to swim with dolphins." I had envisioned being in the water with them for years. Now, my time had come to experience the reality of being in their presence. Little did I know, at the time, that the Law of Attraction was already revealing its amazing power: my desired intention summoned my destiny. Traveling alone was scary, but the ecstatic thoughts of being with beloved dolphins outweighed any fear. And I was blessed to meet incredible angels in human form everywhere I journeyed.

Soon, I was on a cruise ship to the Bahamas to swim with the dolphins in a secluded lagoon. A long boat ride took me and five other dolphin lovers to our destination, where we were led across a wooden bridge. As three dolphins curiously eyeballed their new visitors, I could feel my heart pounding with anticipation. There was no guarantee wild dolphins would swim with me if they weren't in the mood. Dolphins have the unique ability to read the rhythm of our hearts with sonar, and usually won't approach if they are beating too fast. I slowed my breathing down and sent the dolphins love from my heart.

One dolphin named Princess studied me playfully. There was a non-verbal exchange between us, just as there is with humans. The Law of Attraction brought me to Princess. I think Princess knew I had traveled a long way just to be with her. As I slipped into the water, it seemed as if nothing else existed in that moment but Princess and me. As she slowly swam towards me, all I could see was her dorsal fin. I started to feel scared, and reminded myself to breathe. Then, the side of her large muscular body rubbed against my stomach. She was inviting me to play. I laughed from my belly. It felt like I was being transported to another dimension.

Time and space appeared to be suspended as Princess swirled around me in circles. She let me rub her belly, and I experienced a joy I had never known before. The healing properties written about dolphins were true — a feeling of complete well-being ignited every cell of my body. Princess raised her sweet face out of the water and looked right at me. Her telepathic message rang clear in my heart: "You are not alone... I'm here." The deepest feeling of oneness flooded my heart, as if I were a part of something much bigger than myself. I thought, "Dear God, to re-create this moment for others would allow us all to remember Heaven on Earth."

*I thought, "Dear God, to re-create this moment for others would allow us all to remember Heaven on Earth."*

Princess's caretaker instructed me to hold my body perfectly stiff, with my arms held out to my sides. Then, Princess put her forehead beneath my feet and lifted me out of the water as if I were flying. The exhilaration thrilled my soul to no end. I wanted to live in a wetsuit with dolphins for the rest of my life. And I wanted to give back, to share this profound spiritual experience with others. I finally had a knowing that, if I died before I awoke, love would be there to embrace me, with the breath of God to sustain me.

After this incredible healing event, nearly twenty years ago, I prayed for God to use me in creating a place where young and old alike could also be healed of the illusion of separateness and know they are not alone, but one with all of creation. I envisioned providing dolphin-assisted therapy for emotionally and physically challenged people, as well as transformational workshops, entertainment and peace talks between nations in the setting of a world-class eco-resort. Emerald Echo's Dolphin Dynasty would be a place for people to remember who they really are, and rediscover their sense of purpose — a home for nature and mankind to collaborate in a forever friendship. But on my own, this vision remained only a dream.

To prepare for such an undertaking, I went on to earn my master's degree in psychology and worked as a senior social worker while I became a licensed psychotherapist and college professor. I just completed my first children's book *Emerald Echo — The Story*. Emerald Echo is the "echo" inside your heart, inviting you to explore the mystical underwater garden full of treasure, waiting to be discovered.

---

*But on my own, this vision remained only a dream.*

---

It wasn't until I surrendered the dream back to where it originated, in The Heart of God, that my horizons expanded to the concept of cooperative business. Wow! Being part of a team where everyone wins means I get to work with gifted people who are aware of Emerald Echo's magnitude on our planet and are helping to bring it to fruition. Imagine the joy of being in a team where you are able to authentically express your gifts in an environment where power and tenderness meet. It's like swimming with the dolphins! As joyful, playful beings who act as their hearts direct them, dolphins show us the connection and collaboration we are capable of in the mirror of their own graceful rhythms.

As we quiet the mind in sweet stillness, and surrender to our highest calling, the divine can respond above and beyond whatever we had imagined was possible. When we are guided by the Kingdom of Heaven Within, we bring a presence of Heaven on Earth wherever our paths may lead. This is the Law of Attraction in action!

Stepping into a collaborative business model to follow my vision was like walking out of the competitive desert and crossing over to the cooperative land of milk and honey. It was scary quitting a job that promised security and retirement. But in cooperation with priceless friends and colleagues, the dream is now manifesting. Nothing I could have prayed for or planned would have been as extraordinary as the coming together of this moment.

The feeling of immense gratitude for the meaningful connections that have brought me here, now, is like being on the curl of a wave.

*Tamara Bowman, based in Irvine, California, has been a journalist, a saleswoman and a senior social worker. She is now a Licensed Psychotherapist, an author, a Professor of Human Sexuality at Orange Coast College, an inspirational speaker and CEO and founder of Emerald Echo's Dolphin Dynasty. www.tamarabowman.com.*

# Cooperation through Disagreement

LYNN DOHRMANN

As I pressed my head against the cool tiles of the ladies' room, I tried to slow my breathing, and wondered how to get through the meeting that I was about to enter.

In my sixteen years as president of a seminar company that held large multi-media events for several hundred students at a time, I'd had many an anxious moment. Our events were "high-end," so I was putting on an Academy Award-level, live show every other month. Since seminar guests often wait until the last minute to commit, contracting a year in advance for catering and hotel rooms was always difficult. This meeting promised to add to my difficulties.

I walked into the meeting on time, yet all the executive staff of the hotel where my event was being hosted were already seated comfortably around the conference table. As I took my seat, I wished I'd brought one of my staff, so I wouldn't feel so outnumbered. Now, it was too late. I could feel the "them-against-me" air in the room.

"You haven't delivered the number of room nights in your contract," announced the Director of Sales, as he scanned the rooming list, barely glancing up. "You are now in the penalty phase."

"But our event is not over. Many of our attendees are not coming until the weekend," I explained.

"The hotel is sold out for the weekend. We won't be accepting your weekend reservations," he replied.

Lack of cooperation creates anxiety, stress and conflict. In treating me like an adversary, the Director of Sales set up a competitive scenario, which ensured that one of us would win, and one of us would lose. Exasperated, I asked how the hotel could penalize me for failing to produce the required number of attendees while declining reservations from my group that would make up the numbers. Our contract stated that there was *not* a cut-off date for accepting reservations. I cited that important detail, but the sales director just continued to say that our numbers were not in alignment with the contract.

Let me paint a picture of the level of my anxiety. The "penalty" he referred to meant I would be billed an extra five thousand dollars per day for the function space being utilized for my seminar. If I were to say, as a small business owner, that this thirty-five thousand dollar "penalty" over and above my already exorbitant hotel bill for the event was problematic, it would be a quite the understatement. This could be devastating to my business. I could feel my heart pounding as my mind raced into the future, wondering what I would do.

I took another breath and calmly reminded the sales director that our meeting was not concerning a one-time contract, and of the fact that I had been a good client with numerous profitable events in the hotel property. He was unmoved, and we continued in an unproductive dialogue.

---

*Lack of cooperation creates anxiety, stress and conflict. In treating me like an adversary, the Director of Sales set up a competitive scenario, which ensured that one of us would win, and one of us would lose.*

---

The irony was that the seminar we were teaching was about creating win/win situations in business through cooperation. We taught people to work with each other in a manner that honored the human spirit and created long-term results. While these higher-level concepts were being taught in the ballroom, I was in the boardroom getting no cooperation at all, and looking at a lose/lose situation. A non-cooperative mindset is a narrow one that may bring bigger short-term rewards, but in the long run can cost you a fortune.

When I left the meeting, I stopped in the ladies' room again to try to get control of my anxiety. After all, I had to go straight back from this meeting to running my event as if things were going great — and announce the next speaker at the seminar.

Two weeks later, I received the hotel bill and subsequent written notification that I could not host my next, already-scheduled event in the property until the bill (including penalties) was paid in full. I had to negotiate this very difficult situation with a number of conference calls. I believed the penalties to be unfairly and illegally assessed. Our legally binding contract called for "no cut-off date" on accepting reservations, so the hotel's refusal to accept my weekend attendee reservations while assessing penalties to my account was, I believed, easily challenged legally.

However, I could not afford to get into a long-term legal battle over the contract terms. I could not afford the time and money involved to try to prove my legal position. I had to find a way to work with the hotel even though I did not agree with the penalty assessment.

*A non-cooperative mindset is a narrow one that may bring bigger short-term rewards, but in the long run can cost you a fortune.*

I discovered it was important, when feeling attacked, to find a balance between the "lock and load" vs. "duck and cover" mind sets. Because I believed my position was "right," I could have easily gotten into a legal dispute that could have cost much more time and money than accepting the penalty and moving forward.

Finally, the hotel agreed to accept the penalty payments over a longer period while allowing me to host my upcoming events in the property. As soon as the contracts were up for that year, I moved my business to another hotel chain.

The sales director relocated, and a couple years later I was contacted about coming back to the hotel where I'd had so much conflict. This time I met with an amazingly cooperative sales manager, Daniel, who was not only interested in maximizing the hotel's revenue but creating a win/win situation for my company as well. On the dates when his hotel property could not accommodate my group, he personally assisted me with visiting other properties in the area that would work with us in the same cooperative spirit. Daniel and I became friends, and when he changed employment I moved our multimillion-dollar account with him.

A cooperative approach builds long-term relationships that can prosper for years to come. After 9/11/2001, the hotel chain I was using had as much difficulty filling rooms as I had filling seminar seats. They offered us a reduced rate for the upcoming year's events. Then, as our business picked up, I contacted the sales manager and offered to sign new contracts for an increased rate. I knew business had improved for them as well, but I wanted them to be happy our group was coming in, not concerned that they had given us too low a price. I wanted our businesses to thrive together. And as much as I appreciated their graciousness in difficult times, I didn't want to hold them to a rate that now seemed inappropriately low. The sales manager had never had a client volunteer to accept a rate increase.

*A cooperative approach builds long-term relationships that can prosper for years to come.*

Our businesses grew together in a great relationship built on give and take — not sticking strictly to contracted terms, but helping each other through the slow times and sharing the rewarding higher-revenue times.

The difficulty I had worked through years before stayed with me as an example of how frustrating it can be when one is unwilling to compromise in disagreements — and ultimately, it gave me more compassion and empathy when working with others through their own challenges.

*Lynn Dohrmann, a successful business leader, co-founded and served as editor of a national magazine based in California and New York. Lynn operated a public relations company serving the aerospace and defense industry in Huntsville, Alabama, before co-founding the national educational seminar company she served as President for over sixteen years.*

*Lynn is currently working with doctors and other health professionals to impact the wellness profiles of individuals interested in improving their health and longevity. Lynn resides in Madison, Alabama, and may be contacted through her website, www.lynn4water.com.*

# Coming Full Circle

## How I Manifested My Vision through Faith, Planning and Teamwork

MARY CHAN

When I was a little girl, I loved to watch fashion shows on television. I would sit on the living room floor, my eyes glued to the screen. Nothing and no one could tear me away from the elegant models wearing beautiful garments, walking confidently across the stage. I admired their poise, their refinement and their presence. A tornado could have blown by our house, and I would still be watching the show, my eyes glued to the screen.

As a young girl growing up in Edmonton, I could not imagine ever having the courage to be in a fashion show. I was shy, which was sort of a life requirement for young girls in a traditional Chinese culture. I never spoke out of turn, never offered my opinion and never drew attention to myself. Thus, in school I was too shy to raise my hand, even if I knew the answer to a question. Even if I wanted to try something, or ask something or volunteer for something, I kept quiet. Opportunities for learning, fun, and friendship passed me by. Until one day, my parents enrolled me in some personal development programs.

With each class I gained a piece of myself. I came out of my shell. I found my own voice. I was transformed. My self-esteem shot through the roof and there was no stopping me. Gone was the timid, quiet girl afraid to speak up. In her place was my genuine self, confident, ready to go out into the world and test my true potential. Like the models in the fashion shows I adored, I had learned how to present my best self to the world. I was not afraid to be seen or heard. I was not afraid to ask for something I wanted. And I most certainly was not afraid to raise my hand.

Inspired by my interests and my experiences in personal development and fashion production, I started putting on my own events.

It wasn't long before, with the help of my family, I launched Chan International with the goal of creating world-class events.

From a young age I have been blessed to have a clarity of vision, the ability to take a seed idea and bring it to fruition. I know with absolute certainty that I will pursue everything with passion and dedication. It is my unwavering faith that has made it possible for me to accomplish great things — and small things, too!

When I get an idea I sit for hours, often an entire day, putting a plan together to make it happen. In a trance I put the plan together visually, like a business plan, detailing the tasks, the timelines, the job duties and responsibilities. I have to be able to see it, feel that it is in alignment with my values and passion and know that the purpose is positive and geared toward giving back in some way. When all of these things are in place and written down, I can go for it. Before I've told anyone about my idea, I go to work on my plan. That way, when I share the idea with potential partners or team members, I have the plan all ready to go. Creating the plan yields amazing results. The process of building the plan goes way beyond creating a vision board of end goals and concepts. It's the vision and the action steps all in one flowing through my mind systematically.

*I was not afraid to be seen or heard. I was not afraid to ask for something I wanted. And I most certainly was not afraid to raise my hand.*

Little did I know that I was tapping in to the Law of Attraction, and in a big way! Chan International was built on my childhood dreams and from my desire to help people become their true and best selves. We offered classes in personal development similar to the classes I had taken as a young girl.

It was thrilling to see so many people come through our school, confident in themselves and ready to pursue their heart's desires.

Our company was receiving so much attention, and with a waiting list for classes, our business was growing fast. I had envisioned a place for people to reach their full potential through faith, hard work and collaboration with experts; I was able to make that dream a reality.

*I decided to follow my instincts and embrace my true self. I knew I could handle it. More than that, I knew I would be great at it.*

About five years into producing fashion events, I heard a rumor that Madison Square Gardens was looking for a new National Director on behalf of Canada for the Miss Universe pageant (later taken on by Donald Trump's organization). It was a coveted position that required a stringent application process and attracted hundreds of qualified applicants. Even with my experience in production, my chances of getting the position were slim, at best.

But then I remembered all of those times I hadn't raised my hand. I thought, "They have to pick somebody. Why not me?" I decided to follow my instincts and embrace my true self. I knew I could handle it. More than that, I knew I would be great at it.

Using my system for manifesting my vision, I created a detailed proposal and sent it to the Miss Universe organization for review. Not only did I get the job, I held that position for ten years!

Being part of the fashion industry and creating major events provided a platform for me. I became a role model in my industry, so that when I did raise my hand, my voice was heard. With that work behind me, I shifted my focus to my next big dream, a dream that had been brewing for quite some time: to change the world by helping people change themselves.

And so I came full circle, creating the Power of You seminars. My team and I set a goal to produce events on a global level, events that would help people find their purpose in life. We wanted participants to gain all the insight and tools they would need to set out on a mission that was authentic to them, aligned with their values and innermost passion. With my new venture I have come full circle: I went back to the source of my own success to create transformational experiences for others.

Aligned with my true calling, I have attracted an amazing team, one of the best I have ever had the privilege to be part of—and that's saying something, because I have worked with many fantastic teams. The spirit of collaboration is so vital in building a team and for achieving dynamic results.

The synergy of everyone working together outstrips anything that any one person can do by going it alone. You cannot be an expert in everything. Through cooperative business, we can draw together the best-of-the-best people to make one unit moving toward one common goal. We only limit our potential when we try to do everything ourselves.

I believe that I am able to attract people for projects like these because I have faith in my vision. I can see it, feel it, write it down. And then I do it. I start with faith, then I visualize the outcome and plan out every last detail, and when I need someone to fill a specific position, that someone seems to show up out of nowhere. Of course, once you attract people to your project, you still have to get a "yes," which requires that you have a strong sense of self and purpose; you need to boldly present your ideas. To pull together a great team you must first believe in yourself.

---

*We only limit our potential when we try to do everything ourselves.*

---

Would I be me, confident, enthusiastic me, if I had not been given the gift of personal development at such a young age? Probably not. Which is why my exciting new adventures in self-development feel so right — it is the culmination of a lifelong quest to reach my own potential and help others do the same. It's my turn to give back. I always knew I would come full circle. And I have.

*Mary Chan's mandate is to promote a positive self-image above all else. Chan is President of Chan International, a personal development and modeling school, talent agency, and production house based in Alberta, Canada.*

*A producer of numerous world-class events including the International Designer and Fashion Congress in Beijing and Shanghai, China, and the World Fashion Congress in London, England, Mary served as the National Director for the Canadian Search for Miss Universe for ten years. While with Miss Universe, she organized events in Cyprus, Greece, Trinidad and Tobago, Mexico City, Manila and major cities in the United States.*

# Cooperation from a Christian Point of View

DONALD C. MANN

"Here are your tickets," said my boss. I stood in his office, glancing out the window onto a rain-soaked day. "You leave tomorrow for our Profit Drain Division. You can hire or fire anybody you want, and if you don't turn it around, that entire division is gone. You have two months to show results." He turned his attention to something on his desk, so I started out the door; he looked up to add, "Oh yeah. Have a nice day!" I couldn't tell if he was being sarcastic or if he meant it.

I walked out of my boss's office and was greeted by another VP. "Hey Don, heard about your new assignment," he said. He shook his head. "I thought you had real potential, but that place has eaten more people than you can imagine. I hope you make it." He patted my shoulder sympathetically and moved on.

He was right. The Profit Drain Division had swallowed people whole. It had failed to make annual sales and profit goals for the previous three years. It was so bad that chief customers were filing lawsuits against it. Yet the people who worked there were convinced they were the heart of our company. Not one of them thought they would be fired, or that the division could be sold or closed. They were aware of problems, but each of them thought the problems were someone else's fault. Cooperation requires people to be just as open to, and aware of, their weaknesses as they are their strengths.

On the short walk back to my office, as I processed all of this, I fully grasped the enormity of the job ahead. I had to enter an environment of fear, counterproductive competitiveness and obvious failure and somehow make it successful. I started to feel daunted by the idea, so when I got to my office I did what believers do: I called on the Lord Jesus

Christ with a big, one-word prayer: "What?" After my prayer, I realized that this challenge was, in fact, an opportunity that could be a career-defining moment. I determined to find a way to make this work without firing anyone. I knew that if there was a solution to this problem, I would find it, provided I kept my heart open to God's guidance.

What help could I expect? Would God cooperate with me to make this work? Or is it the other way around? A Christian is someone in whom the Holy Spirit dwells, the same Holy Spirit that dwells in Jesus Christ. A Christian is a different kind of creature. If you are a Christian, the Spirit of the Living God dwells in you because of your faith that Jesus' blood paid for all sin and that God raised Jesus Christ from the dead. To believe in this is to be "born again." Since I was a Christian, I realized that I could expect as much help from God as I needed. But I also had to ask for it. Part of cooperation is letting your partner know what you need, so I had to let God know what I needed. The ultimate level of cooperation is to operate as a co-worker with God through the Holy Spirit to bring heaven to earth. Our fullest potential is achieved when we cooperate with our Creator — within ourselves — to help us bring true good into the world.

*Cooperation requires people to be just as open to, and aware of, their weaknesses as they are their strengths.*

The Christian life is one that uses the Holy Spirit in order to do His work on earth. The goals for a Christian are simple: fix anything that is not like heaven; improve what is already working well and strive to do everything as Jesus would. A Christian, uniquely, has the Holy Spirit abiding within; but a Christian must still cooperate with God to create heaven on earth. That cooperation is about more than just walking in God's ways for one's own benefit. It is about living for others at the same time. The Bible, the Word of God, is the pathway of right thinking and action, which allows God to enter the Earth. But because of the death and the resurrection of Jesus, the Holy Spirit can also come alive from within us, and it's that Holy Spirit that can make all things new and bring miraculous creativity to all tasks.

But — time was short. I quickly gathered all the reports, completed travel arrangements, developed a transition plan for my current business units and immersed myself into the world of my new assignment. On my drive home that night, I praised God for His goodness and this opportunity to confront my own Goliath. I knew it wasn't going to be an easy battle. We are not promised an easy journey. Jesus and the saints show us that. What we are promised is present victory and ultimate triumph with lots of hard work and many "fear storms" in between.

The Bible says, "Praise is comely for the upright." On my forty-five minute drive home, I started singing and shouting Psalm 23 phrases, one of my favorites for praise and battles. Then I began praying, singing and shouting in tongues (one of the gifts of the Holy Spirit). My habit is to aim for at least one hour a day in tongues, usually as I drive to and from work. I had discovered over the years that when I do this, I usually end up doing the right things in the right way. Our job is to extend His love on the earth; we are promised that He will help us stand and fight the enemy of our souls.

As I pray and trust through praise, He will guide me to do the right things and give me favor. The answers are not always quick and easy, and they don't always come exactly when I want them, but they come, and they are right.

On my new assignment, my role was to coach my new team to release the answers we needed. The Bible says more than 365 times, and in many different ways, "Be not afraid; I am with you to help you." God warns us that fear will constantly assault us. My first task was to remove fear and establish goals of performance. I had to get my team to buy into the vision that if it could be done, we would do it. Ours was the only technology of its kind in the entire world, and it was up to us to fix its reliability and profitability.

I set a few rules:

- We shoot no messengers, and everyone gets his or her say. Silence is fine, but it is counted as acceptance and is held accountable as such. No backbiting is allowed.
- We keep the vision in mind. Every meeting has an agenda, a project plan and a status of current items, with assignments and due dates. All stakeholders and decision makers are involved, all sub-tasks are managed and all results are communicated to the entire team. Ignorance is unacceptable.
- There is no clock, only results. We work as long as it takes and as long as it is safe (some of this technology was very dangerous). We manage to meet schedules and commitments.
- We recognize, praise and reward good work and results. All other limiting behaviors are ignored or, as necessary, dealt with individually. The only fear allowed is that of negative consequences for not being fully committed to getting optimal results. Otherwise, every failure or unexpected result is just another challenge to be solved.
- We invent what we need to make this a success. (In many cases we had to invent solutions to solve the problems, so that was also added to the project plan. I really counted on this rule, since one of the hallmarks of the reformed Christian era is invention and innovation.)

We did it! With people who'd been failing for three years, we took a struggling twenty-five million dollar business and created over five-hundred million in value. We created new technologies, started new businesses, and became a world standard in excellence. But there were other, more lasting results. As per 1 John 4:1–4, I got very good at trusting my gut, my intuition. I also developed solid business relationships with some of the best minds on the planet, and a few have become lifelong friends. All of this was the result of implementing the cooperative attitude. In Moses' time, God clearly articulated the principle of cooperation in Leviticus 19:18, and in Matthew 22:37–40, Jesus reiterated it: "Thou shalt love the Lord thy God with all thy heart, and with all thy soul, and with all thy mind. This is the first and great commandment. And the second is like unto it, Thou shalt love thy neighbor as thyself. On these two commandments hang all the law and the prophets."

So my turnaround of this division was based on God's solid path of treating others as I wanted to be treated. God told Adam to "subdue and establish dominion" because the world outside the Garden of Eden needed fixing. Jesus came as the last Adam to get the Holy Spirit inside of us by faith in the power of His blood. The result is that both the natural and the supernatural aspects of God become one inside a Christian. That awesome potential for creative good is in us. It is released as we cooperate with God, through the pathways of the Holy Spirit and the Bible, to "fix" the earth. Turning that failing division around provided valuable products and kept a town fed for years, a very valid set of "good works" based on the power of cooperation and the laws of abundance.

These laws work whether you are a Christian or not, for God wants good to come to any who will work with Him. A good man and a bad man can both plant a seed of corn and, if they care for it properly, see abundance. Cooperation is one of those laws available to all, and it produces the best fruit for all.

*Don Mann advises CEOs and business leaders across the globe. In organizations ranging from start-ups to Fortune 100s, he has delivered improved innovation, sales, profits and cash flow in good and hard times. His results include developing and improving highly productive — and lean — organizations, which now see quicker responsiveness, reduced stress and profitable customer delight. Sitting on a number of boards, he helps CEOs grow their companies and shareholder value. For more information, contact him at www.ritemann.com*

# Teaming Up To Save Families

DEBORAH CHAN

Deeply touched by Jeffrey Sachs's book *The End of Poverty*, my mission in life has been to serve the one billion people on the planet who live in extreme poverty. Most of them live in Africa, China and India. However, poverty and other less extreme financial crises exist in the United States as well, and often in places you may not expect to find them.

George was seventy years old when he got laid off. He lived with his wife and disabled son, and they all needed money to see them through the rest of their lives. So George decided to sell his share of a building he owned. The timing was perfect — George's investment partner found someone right away who wanted to buy out his share in the building. George was reluctant to sell, however, because it meant he would have to pay a large sum in capital gains tax.

George was in a typical real estate bind. Upon the sale of highly appreciated real estate with significant capital gains, many folks use a 1031-exchange strategy to defer capital gains tax by acquiring another like-kind piece of real estate. But George and his family needed the cash.

I'm a real estate investment advisor and wealth strategist with my own practice, Maven Wealth Strategies. I also work with the Estate Planning Team™, an association of tax attorneys, estate attorneys, CPAs, real estate brokers, life insurance agents, financial advisors, investment advisors and money managers committed to helping people protect their estates and preserve their wealth. We have a powerful tool and perfect solution for George: the Deferred Sales Trust™, or DST.

The DST is an alternative to the 1031-exchange. It's legal but complex. Here's how it works: a DST allows real estate investors to sell property to a designated trust. Over time, the trust pays back the seller in the form of an installment sales note. Then the trust sells the property to the end-buyer. Any capital gains tax is deferred until repayment is received (over the period of the installment note). Working in a collaborative environment, my team members and I are able to make this complex solution available to everyday people and families. That's what I love about DSTs — the fact that they require a team to work together for a common goal. When I work with DSTs, I become part of a team focused on helping people.

---

*Working collaboratively and collectively as one team, and as one with the Universe, a special vibration energized us all.*

---

A DST is effective, and powerful. My team has already used DSTs to help approximately 4,600 clients. A DST can generate substantially more wealth over the long run than a direct or taxed sale, and in terms of estate planning, it will help generations to come. That's what it did for George. We had to work fast, which is usually the case when forming a DST. My team did work expeditiously, often late into the night, but our efforts over the course of a week saved George and his family a lot of money. Working collaboratively and collectively as one team, and as one with the Universe, a special vibration energized us all.

I got into advisory services because I love helping and serving people. Money, to me, is a means and not an end. Money is just a tool that, when used wisely, can help us solve problems and enable us to live a comfortable life. Real happiness is not found in building ever-larger, unused toolboxes, but by using the tools we do have to live lives that reflect our values. So the more money we have — spent wisely and with clear intent — the more comfort and abundance there is to go around, and the better able we are to manifest our dreams. Positive energy always radiates outward.

All too often, though, potential positive energy is blocked by circumstance. "If I sell my property, I'm going to get killed with taxes."

I hear sentiments like that all the time. People often want to sell their properties, but threats of impending taxes stifle their plans. Taxes are necessary, but sometimes those who create them do not know — and cannot know — individual taxpayer circumstances, or how burdensome taxes can be and how they can potentially stop the flow of energy and prevent freedom of choice.

If a property is not sold, the change that could have nourished everything and everyone involved — buyer, seller, agents, escrow officers, interior designers, contractors, tenants, property managers, the neighborhood and the property itself — never occurs.

If you want more of something in your life — whether it's money, love, appreciation, attention or kindness — you need to keep it flowing. As Deepak Chopra said in his book *The Seven Spiritual Laws of Success*, to attract more wealth we need to *circulate* our wealth. The word "affluence" comes from the French word *affluere*, "to flow to," and the word "currency" is derived from the Latin *currere*, "to run" or "to flow." Do you see how wealth is a natural result of being in the universal flow?

So with the DST tool and a qualified, dedicated team to make it work, we *activate* a creative energy through which change occurs and lives are improved. We help people access the universal flow, attracting abundance.

I am part Japanese, and the Japanese have a word that is very important to me: *keiretsu*. It essentially means synergy, joining forces to work for mutual benefit. I believe in this principle; I practice and live it. Cooperative business benefits everyone involved. When my team helped George, we were not focused on what each of us could get. Instead, we focused on serving and empowering George and his family. And because giving was the focus, we all benefited. We were all giving, and so we all received. It is in the giving that we receive.

I believe there is a vibrational frequency in giving and sharing, a frequency that emanates outward but always comes back. It may not appear to reverberate immediately — it could take months, or years. But the more we open up, the more awakened we are to life's opportunities and gifts, the more that energy spreads through giving. It spreads to everyone in our orbit and comes back expanded, energizing us even further.

*In competition, there are winners and losers.*
*In collaboration, there are only winners.*

It's this kind of environment and energy that attracts clients and colleagues to us. People are naturally inclined to work together. Conversely, being competitive goes against our nature and drains us of vital energy. Competition, from a spiritual perspective, is not particularly conducive to growth, and real estate is one of the most competitive businesses out there. There is a lot of mistrust, miscommunication and misunderstanding among real estate professionals (unless there is an established history of trusting relationships). I have never liked the cutthroat nature of the business. That's part of the reason I wanted to create my own entity, my own practice that would embody my working principles, values and philosophies. In competition, there are winners and losers. In collaboration, there are only winners.

My friend Ken is a realtor and advisor working for Pacific Union. Ken has a monthly newsletter to which he invited me to submit an article on DSTs. I did, and we both benefited. I gained more exposure, and he gained more credibility as a realtor and advisor because the article showed he was in touch with the newest trends in real estate investment strategies. And, our professional relationship — as well as our friendship — was strengthened by this collaboration.

Teamwork is also incredibly empowering for us and for our clients. Recently, I gave a presentation at a global expo for real estate investors in San Jose. My team asked Dustin, one of our estate planning attorneys, to co-present with me. Even though we'd given him very short notice, he flew up and joined me without hesitation.

We had a great audience, and they asked many intelligent questions. With his extensive legal and tax knowledge, Dustin was able to answer questions thoroughly and with ease. He was really technical, detailed and credible. Had I been on my own, I would not have been able to answer some of the audience's questions. I would have had to tell them that I would get back to them later with accurate answers. I was immensely grateful Dustin was there.

Our joint efforts always provide us with more credibility. Whenever our team works together, we can answer the most difficult of questions relating to complicated transactions or unique scenarios. In identifying our strengths and weaknesses, and seeking out the help of those who have the knowledge and experience we lack, we build trustworthy teams, teams that — together — provide better products for our clients. Working together in a harmonious team, we improve the lives of others and empower them with revolutionary tools like the DST.

We improve financial lives and therefore livelihoods; we help provide more comfort, and everyone involved benefits. The more we operate as a team in our families, our businesses and our communities, the more peace, love and joy we will provide for the good of humanity.

*Deborah Chan,* CEO *of Maven Wealth Strategies, is a licensed California real estate broker and life-licensed agent. She educates, empowers and enriches people, businesses and companies with cutting edge, innovative wealth strategies, most of them unknown to Americans. One of these wealth strategies is the Deferred Sales Trust™ from the Estate Planning Team™.*

*In 2001 Deborah was named "Queen" for raising the most money that year for the oldest non-profit in San Francisco, The Little Jim Club of California Pacific Medical Center. The organization raises funds to support pre-natal, neo-natal and child development programs at the hospital. To learn more about Deborah, visit www.mavenwealth.com and www.creative1031.com.*

# Conclusion

## by Ruby Yeh

This is just the beginning ...

The true stories in this book reveal the immense power of two. Two — or twenty, or two hundred — move faster, better and more efficiently than one. A group of individuals enlightened to the *limitless possibilities* of working collaboratively can do extraordinary things — they can do the impossible. Having read this book, you have ignited a spark of inspiration in your heart, which when acted upon, will set your business, your life, and your future "on fire."

In reading the illuminating tales of cooperative business in action, you may have become aware of the ways in which you already operate this way. Perhaps you are a natural collaborator like me and your beliefs about business were confirmed in reading the methodologies explored in this book. Or maybe you are new to these concepts, and now have a notebook full of ideas, or at least a vision for what is possible for your business.

---

*Having read this book, you have ignited a spark of inspiration in your heart, which when acted upon, will set your business, your life, and your future "on fire."*

---

Something attracted you to this book — perhaps a desire to experience more joy in your work. Or, maybe thoughts of the abiding dream you carry around with you motivated you to seek out ways for your dream to finally take flight. The same force that attracted you to this book will, when tapped into through collaboration, attract new business to you: new revenue, new opportunities, new ideas, new partners, new investors and new customers.

---

*The same force that attracted you to this book will, when tapped into through collaboration, attract new business to you: new revenue, new opportunities, new ideas, new partners, new investors and new customers.*

---

How can you harness and cultivate this energy in your own life? Where can you gather with other like-minded people, gain support and transform your business? The authors of this book are all members of CEO Space. To learn more about this powerful group, please visit www.CEOSpace.net.

The revolution is just beginning. Are you ready?

We invite you to also enjoy
*The Law of Business Attraction* multi-media book.

It's an online version of this book, and with it you can hear and see the authors through audio and video.

As a gift, we're offering you a chance to read over twenty pages of the multi-media book at:

www.LawOfBusinessAttraction.com

If you wish to buy the complete multi-media copy, please use this coupon code to receive a substantial discount.

Coupon Code – Book1

If you would like to meet like-minded entrepreneurs and business leaders like the authors in this book, they are all members of an unique and powerful collaborative organization called CEO Space.

Learn more at www.CEOSpace.net